A N D   M E

The Real Bob Marley Story
Told by his manager **DON TAYLOR**
With **MIKE HENRY**

BARRICADE BOOKS
Fort Lee, N.J.

Published by Barricade Books Inc.

www.barricadebooks.com
by arrangement with Kingston Publishers Ltd.

Printed in the United States of America.

Library of Congress Cataloging-in-Publication Data
Taylor, Don.
Marley and me: by Don Taylor as told to Mike Henry.
p. cm.
ISBN 1-56980-044-8 (pbk.): $15.95
1.Marley, Bob. 2. Singers—Jamaica—Biography. 3. Reggae musicians—Jamaica—
Biography. I. Henry, Mike (L. Michael) II. Title.
ML420.M3313T39 1994
782.42164—dc20

[B]   94-45789
         CIP
         MN

13th Printing

In memory of Kyle Donald Taylor

1988–1993

and the birth of Miles Joseph Taylor

August 1994.

C O N T E N T S

THE WORLD

SCAVENGERS

ACKNOWLEDGMENTS

■ could never have achieved the successes I have had were it not for the following people, beginning with my early years as a promoter and on through the present.

To the following I acknowledge my sincere appreciation: Stephen Hill, Sr.; the R & B family of 1958 to 1968; Ben E. King; Jerry Butler; Chuck Jackson;, the late Jackie Wilson; the Shirelles—especially Shirley Owens; Walter Godfrey; the Drifters; the late Tammi Montgomery Terrell; Betty Everett; Little Anthony and the Imperials—especially Anthony Gourdine; that great contributor Henry Wynn, who was the guiding light at "sweet" Auburn Avenue; Bobby Schiffman, owner of the Apollo; and Murray the K, "fifth Beatle," who was responsible for so many shows at the Brooklyn Fox; to Patti La Belle and the Blue Belles; Dick Griffey; Kendal Minter; Vivian Scott; Danny Sims; Janet Davidson and Jackie Davidson; and in later years, the Top Line crew of Marcia Davis, Bagga Davis, and my close confidante, Danny Marks. Thanks to all the "Wise Guys" that I have met and worked with in the world, for being "standup" people. I would also say thanks to Mrs. Irwin Marsh, Nari and Hotu Chatani, Nicky Nicholas, Tom Tavares-Finson, and my other mother, Aunt Daisy Belizario.

In the life of my association with Bob, special thanks to all those who played a part in his success and indeed, by extension, my own success. In this category I place Chris Blackwell, Rita Marley, Cedella Booker, Judy Mowatt, Marcia Griffiths, the Wailers band, "Family Man" Barrett, Carlton Barrett, Tyrone Downie, Alvin "Seco" Patterson, Al Anderson, Junior Marvin, Alex Sadkin (deceased), King Sporty, Captain Curry, and of course, Bob's children. I will be forever grateful to Bunny Livingston and Peter Tosh who together with Bob formed the original Wailers; without them I would have no story to tell today. Thanks also to Frankie Crocker of WBLS, New York, and all DJs and program directors, and all the Island Record licensees around the world, who played their part in building Bob's career. I am also immensely grateful to April Taylor, my former wife, who did so much for Bob while he stayed with us in Miami.

With respect to the book itself, I must pay special thanks to coauthor Mike Henry and to Camille Hines-Henry for bringing Mike and me together to make this book a reality. Many thanks also to Dawn Chambers who transcribed the tapes as I recorded them, spending endless hours typing and retyping. To Abe Dabdoub for his legal advice and Dwight and Christine Simons of WRR. Special thanks to Kim Robinson-Walcott for her incisive editorial advice, editor Annie Paul who helped to bring coherence to the manuscript, and to Susan Anderson for her work on the book, as well.

I wish to acknowledge the role played in my research by such publications as *Catch a Fire* by Timothy White, *Bob Marley: Reggae King of the World* by Malika Whitney (a former secretary of mine) and Dermot Hussey, *Reggae International* by Stephen Davis and Peter Simons, *In His Own Words* (Omnibus Publishers), *Reggae Report* magazine (owned by Peggy

Quattro, also a former secretary of mine), and the *Daily Gleaner*.

My eternal thanks to the medical fraternity who saved my life. I refer specifically to Dr. William Bacon of Miami, Florida, and Dr. Phillip Thompson of Nassau, Bahamas. And finally, I must thank my wife Sonia, who has shared the birth of this book.

Don Taylor

PRELUDE: MIAMI 1980

Bob Marley was seething with rage, his eyes simmering like a wild mountain cat's. Never before had I ever seen him in such a fury.

Slowly he cocked the trigger of the huge, black, automatic 9mm pistol and leveled the muzzle inches from my right eye. Behind him, armed with an identical gun, loomed his road manager, Allan Cole.

"Sign the paper Don Taylor or I am going to blow you away," Bob whispered. "Just do it man."

I read the document he waved in my face: it dissolved every verbal and written agreement made between the two of us over the years.

I had dedicated years of my life to Bob's career, helping him, in a small way, to grow from a ghetto "Tuff Gong" to a poised, respected, multi-millionaire global superstar. Now he was trying to undo everything between us—everything I had worked for—in an act of betrayal.

The afternoon had started routinely enough with a call from Bob, who was staying at his mother's mansion in Miami between concert tours of Europe and the Far East. He had asked me to come over to chat about something that was worrying him. We began our talk by his huge, shimmering swimming pool. As the conversation grew more and more heated, he commanded Allan and me to move to his room.

Within minutes the three of us were scuffling, and Allan had drawn two evil-looking pistols out of a wooden bedroom wardrobe.

Even with the guns pointed at me, I tried to stay cool. Not that I wasn't frightened—it occurred to me that Bob just might shoot. But I also understood the old Jamaican technique of intimidation. Like Bob I'd grown up battering about on the streets of Jamaica and understood how Jamaicans used intimidation to get their way. I also knew that the bluster and threats rarely led to bloodshed.

Bob continued screaming and waving the gun at me, "You're going to sign—what you trying to do to me?"

I met his threatening stare defiantly and told him, "I'm not going to sign."

At that moment one of the small children, I think it was Ziggy, appeared in the doorway.

"Don and Daddy fighting!" he shouted to his grandmother.

Bob suddenly calmed down. He respected his mother and would do nothing to upset her.

When I finally parted with Bob on that decisive day, I noticed that his moods seemed to be growing more and more unpredictable. I also left knowing that my relationship with him was over.

We had both ascended so far from our humble beginnings that for either of us there was simply no going back. He had risen from the slums of Trench Town in Jamaica to become a worldwide superstar, a global icon of liberation movements.

I, too, had undertaken my own odyssey that began with my thirteen-year-old mother going into labor in Jamaica's Victoria Jubilee Hospital . . .

BEGINNINGS

1

GROWING UP IN JAMAICA
— WATERFRONT VERSION

I was born in Jamaica on a typical cloudless, sunlit day on February 10th, 1943, arriving at just about the time the island's most influential newspaper, the *Gleaner*, was being tossed onto the manicured lawns of the uptown homes.

I'm told that it was a bright, sparkling day fit for a tourist brochure, the kind that Bob Marley would sing about:

> *Sun is shining, the weather is sweet*
> *Make you want to move your dancing feet*
> *When the morning gather the rainbow*
> *Want you to know, I'm a rainbow too*
> ("Sun is Shining")

My mother, Cynthia Llewellyn, thirteen years old and a black maid, had given birth to me at the Victoria Jubilee Hospital, one of twenty newborns born in the hospital that Wednesday in 1943.

Kingston, the capital of Jamaica and my birthplace, had seen many changes since its founding in 1692, when the island's former capital, Port Royal, was destroyed in an earthquake. At the time of my birth as now, the city retained its original seventeenth century grid-like physical layout, bounded on three sides by North, East and West Streets, and on the south by the Kingston harbor. In true colonial style, the main arteries of the city were named King, Queen, Duke and Hanover Streets.

Franklin Town, where I lived and was raised in the eastern end of the city, was a grid of dimly lit, narrow, crisscrossing streets. Its spacious Victorian houses were occupied by renters, the well-off owners having fled the city for the foothills of St. Andrew to escape the flood of poor Jamaicans pouring in from the countryside.

Here I spent the first ten years of my life as Donald Kidd.

My mother, whom I never really knew either then or in later years, was living at my birth with a black gardener named Taylor. Even so, she had had a brief affair with Vernal Kidd, a white British soldier stationed at the Up Park Camp barracks, which was then an English barracks but is now the home of the Jamaica Defense Force.

As the story goes, after my birth Mr. Taylor became suspicious and questioned my mother sharply about my fair complexion, but somehow she always managed to convince him that, given time, I would properly darken.

Nine months later with Mr. Taylor asking troublesome questions about my complexion again, my mother abruptly took me to Up Park Camp and deposited me on the desk of my biological father, Mr. Vernal Kidd.

My newly found father was Scottish and in charge of the motor pool of his regiment. We never became close, and after the first ten years I didn't see him again until 1969.

Mr. Kidd, or "Kidd" as everyone in Franklin Town knew him, promptly began looking for someone with whom he

could leave me. It was a search that was to continue throughout the first ten years of my life.

One day he took me to the home of Mrs. Minnie Malabre,
who apparently had no children. I vividly remember how Mrs.
Malabre led me by the hand to the back verandah (a common
feature of the houses at the time), making it clear that as a bastard with black mother who was a maid, I was not good
enough for the front of her house.

His attempt to pawn me off on Mrs. Malabre having failed,
Mr. Kidd eventually succeeded with Aunt Daisy Belizario who
resided at Cambridge Street. Aunt Daisy was one of those rare
"brown" Jamaican ladies of English descent and good breeding who had fallen on hard times. Although only a petite four
feet eleven inches tall, she always carried herself with dignity
and pride. Kind, soft-spoken, and gentle, she was not much
given to histrionics.

Because Aunt Daisy also looked after four other children
born under similar circumstances, her day-to-day living was
built on the theme of "God will provide." And she was right,
too. God did provide where my Mr. Kidd didn't.

Many were the desperate days Aunt Daisy would scribble
a note, stick it in my hand, and send me off to an importer who
ran a business on Orange Street in downtown Kingston. I
would return with an envelope of money. The note to the
importer never failed, although to this day I don't know why.

By the time I was eleven, however, Aunt Daisy had just
about given up on me. She could not keep me in school, no
matter how hard she tried, for I had been spending all my days
on the waterfront.

The Kingston waterfront was then a hive of exciting activity. Not a week passed when there was not a US or British

naval vessel in port. Cruise ships made scheduled stops. The United Fruit Company banana boats called to unload cargo for Kingston's merchants and traders before sailing for Port Antonio, Oracabessa and Montego Bay to pick up the bananas for the markets of Britain and the USA.

It was quite a sight for me, a boy of eleven, to see all these ships sailing in and out of one of the world's finest natural harbors—the port of Kingston—whose backdrop was framed by the majestic Blue Mountain range, its wreathed green peak towering over eight thousand feet.

Located along this Kingston waterfront strip was Jamaica's first major hotel, the Myrtle Bank, a palatial edifice that had been built by the United Fruit Company. I would pass this magnificent colonial-style structure almost daily, its elaborate iron fence protecting the expanse of green manicured lawns from native feet, its lawns overlooking the driveway lined by towering swaying royal palms.

To all but rich brown Jamaicans and white tourists, the Myrtle Bank was then forbidden territory. A few years later the late Evon Blake, black author and journalist, would dive head-first into its swimming pool, cause consternation and newspaper headlines, and shatter this exclusivity. Many were the days when, having escorted recent ship passengers to the grounds of the Myrtle Bank, I would watch them stroll casually inside the portals of this fabulous palace, leaving me on the street gawking with envy and longing.

Hotels such as the Myrtle Bank Hotel in Kingston, the Titchfield Hotel and the Ethelhart in Port Antonio, and the Casa Blanca in Montego Bay were then at the core of a budding tourist trade and important to the United Fruit Company whose ships, in addition to transporting bananas to England, also brought visitors to Jamaica.

Eventually, in a move significant for Jamaica's future, the hotel was bought by Arab Jamaican, Abe Issa, the godfather of the tourist industry. This acquisition lead to a fantastically successful career in tourism. Issa moved on to buy Tower Isle (now Couples), in St. Mary, and finally some five more hotels worldwide, leaving behind a legacy and an industry that is today Jamaica's largest foreign exchange earner.

During these apprenticeship days, my life centered around the streets of downtown Kingston that ran parallel and perpendicular to the waterfront. They formed the throbbing pulse of the city.

Here lay the premier commercial shopping areas of Harbor Street and King Street, then the home of the leading Arab and Jewish merchants, whose shops were bursting with imported goods. Here the businesses of the Issas, the Morins, the Duries and the Hannas—the fabulous stores such as Nathans, Morins, Times Store and E.A. Issa & Brothers—competed cheek by jowl with Indian merchants, the Dadlanis and Chatanis with their exquisite jewelry and silk. Here were the street vendors loudly hawking their camphor balls, hair curlers, clothes pins and sweets on the sidewalks.

Some two blocks away, threading a path parallel to King Street from north to south, ran Duke Street, home of the island's major legal firms, with their hushed, wainscoted offices.

But these were only places I had seen in passing or knew about through rumor. My own life was elsewhere, on other streets, and began in earnest only after the thick tropical darkness blanketed the island and Kingston was blazing in its nighttime glitter.

Then you would find me in the bars and clubs scattered among the dimly lit streets of downtown Kingston, from east to west and north to south. West Street housed the renowned Fats Waller All American Bar, which had recently relocated from Hanover Street to become the first bar homesick sailors stumbling ashore would encounter. Hanover Street boasted a glittering string of bars and clubs. Here was Ma Chung's, Captain's Corner and Sailor's Rest.

All these clubs were much the same, inside and out. They all had a wooden bar, with stools of varying heights, sizes and styles. They all had jukeboxes with the latest overseas hits and outside walls festooned with gaudy designs and advertisements painted by untrained local artists.

Inside, the walls were decorated with photographs cut from the pages of US magazines or nude calendars. Scribbled above the bars would be the prevailing business ethic, "Cash is alive. Credit is dead." Back rooms were fitted out with the basic essentials necessary for short-term personal gratification.

The stock in trade of the bar was Jamaican white rum of the highest proof that could scorch the most experienced alcoholic throat. Red rum brands such as Black Seal, Gold Seal and Appleton were sold along with the inimitable Jamaican Red Stripe Beer as well as foreign beer brands such as Pabst Blue Ribbon, Budweiser and Heineken.

The bars all but exclusively catered to the ordinary sailor, soldier and lower-class Jamaican, although occasionally upper-class Jamaicans would stop by on their way home from their offices, or on their way to expensive brothels and whorehouses located in many of these areas of Kingston.

Kingston at this time boasted such exclusive brothels as Strolley's, Dewdney's Paradise Club and Maidman's Bamboo Bar, a bar which was run by an Englishman, who was always referred to as *Mister*. Many of today's businessmen, politicians and columnists were frequent visitors to these brothels, and one or two of the live-in girls have gone on to fame and fortune. There was the usual distinction between the street whores and the live-in ladies.

Because they offered very few economic benefits for me, I very rarely visited any of these upper-class clubs and whorehouses. The bars, on the other hand, did not share the rigid rules of the brothels, and since they were open to the public, it was quite in order for uptowners to visit and partake of the late-night action. Kingston had not yet become segregated by wealth and class as it is today, and in the fifties, all of its citizens moved freely without fear for their safety.

The city, however, was already showing signs of decay, leading the more affluent residents to move into the hills of St. Andrew, abandoning Jones Town, Denham Town and Trench Town to the newly arrived downtrodden and oppressed from the countryside about whom Bob Marley sang in his "Trench Town Rock."

But it was on the waterfront of Kingston where my exposure to life began and where I flourished.

One of the first things you learned in this environment was to be sharp, quick, smart and ready for any break. To be ready for any break usually meant watching for the chance to escape the island, which meant always keeping a valid passport handy just in case the opportunity to migrate to the big outside world ever arose.

It was this ambition to leave that led me to seek out my birth certificate and to discover that my mother had registered me Donald Delroy Taylor, after her live-in gardener. I had his name, but not his color.

By the time I turned thirteen, in 1956, I was four feet tall, and confident enough to face life with a smile. Given the rules of the game, I was learning fast. I hustled day and night among the ranks of the waterfront's slickest hustlers such as Benjie Howard, the top waterfront pimp, noted by his peers for his mode of dress—always in the latest American style and fashion. We all had what I would call a "foreign mind," maybe because our minds were always on the next US buck, and our hearts were always yearning for the exciting worlds of New York and London. Many of the hustlers even spoke with a phony American accent, which I myself never adopted.

I can still visualize such professionals as Dutch and the pier foreman, Mr. Kirlew.

Dutch always dressed like a naval officer, clean, fresh and upright. He would step aboard a recently berthed ship, salute the captain with military precision, and launch into his well-planned marketing spiel that never failed to work. It was characters such as Dutch and Benjie who fine-tuned my antennae, preparing me to face the world with confidence and very few hang-ups.

There was never a dull moment for me on the waterfront, for as the sailors and the cruise passengers disembarked, I became tourist guide, pimp or hustler, depending on their needs and desires. I would, for a fee and a reward, guide them to whatever they wanted. I would take some cruise passengers to the Myrtle Bank Hotel or hustle them into a taxi to ride uptown to the Hope Zoo and Gardens, or further on to Castleton Gardens, some twenty miles into the hills. I preferred, however, to persuade them to follow me to my favorite bars, where I had my private financial deals with the bartenders and the girls.

By sixteen I had come up with a lot of ideas that set me apart from the average hustler. I struck many and varied deals with club owners and waitresses. One such deal was that any beer I ordered would be sold to me for two shillings, and I in turn would sell it for three or four shillings to the unsuspecting sailors. By pre-arrangement, the waiters would refuse to take the sailors' orders except through me. In true hustler style, I got the bar people to realize that they had to cater to me in order to keep the business.

On the days that the ships did not come in, I scrounged for other ways and means to earn a living. Sometimes I would wash the cars of leading businessmen. I remember washing cars in the park at Duke Street for such businessmen as Danny Williams, then working for North American Life Insurance Company; Roy Morin, owner of the best men's department store on King Street; Vivian Blake, leading lawyer and politician who would later challenge Michael Manley for leadership of the PNP (People's National Party) after the retirement of Michael's father, Norman Manley.

By being street-smart and by knowing how to hustle, I was able to survive. I spent most of my nights in the clubs. I knew all the barmaids, waitresses, bartenders, pimps, prostitutes, and gamblers.

Looking back today I still regard those days as among the most enjoyable in my life. The waterfront had become my home, its people replacing the mother and father I had never had. And always lurking in the background was faithful, dependable Aunt Daisy providing a place of refuge when I needed one.

Another of my main means of income was to hustle Lucky Strike and Camel cigarettes from the US sailors and sell them at a good profit to the Chinese, Indian and Syrian merchants and the bars. To buy the cartons, I would often dive for the money thrown overboard by the cruise ship visitors—a favorite pastime for us waterfront boys.

I used to frequent Mr. Hill's kerosene shop on Hanover Street, between Laws and Barry Streets, where at times his son Micky Hill and I would exchange youthful thoughts. Uptown kids were always curious to know how we, the street people, lived.

I remember vividly my only brush with the law, when my friend, if I could call him that, Chiney Man, got me into a tricky situation. Over time I had developed a connection at Wray and Nephew that allowed me to buy rum at a bargain price. On this occasion, Chiney Man ran away with money an American lady had given us to buy her some white rum. She reported the theft to Gupte, an Indian policeman who was openly feared by the waterfront hustlers because he made no bones about sending thieves and pimps to jail. He chased me and held me that Friday and locked me up over the weekend at the Central Police Station. I escaped prison only because of a young lawyer, Noel Silvera, who used to play cricket at Kensington Cricket Club where I hung out in my younger days. He saw me in the Sutton Street Court, knew that I was not totally bad, and agreed to personally pay back the money. The case was dismissed, leaving me eternally in his debt.

My first taste of show business and its personnel came through the Ward Theater, a few blocks from the waterfront, and immediately overlooking the Queen Victoria Park.

Ward Theater was, and still is, Jamaica's premier theater. This impressive concert hall was a gift to the people of Jamaica from Colonel Ward.

One day I was on the waterfront close to the Queen Victoria Pier, with very little to do, as it was not a cruise or warship day. I was looking for action and as fate would have it, I met Lloyd Price, the American singer. Lloyd had already struck gold with his massive hit "Personality" which had brought him to Jamaica. Because of the transistor radio, which had become a status symbol on the waterfront, I knew all about him and his music.

Lloyd Price and I got talking and quickly became friends. When he invited me to visit him at his uptown hotel, the Flamingo Hotel in Cross Roads, I immediately said "yes," eager to learn more about the fascinating world of entertainment. It was during this encounter that I first heard the name Stephen Hill, who had brought Lloyd Price to Jamaica.

During the late fifties Stephen Hill—a medium-height, sharp-featured brown Jamaican like myself—had the reputation of being Jamaica's leading impresario. With his wife Dorothy, Hill had been the Jamaican pioneer of show promotions. He had brought to the island artistes ranging from classical pianist Artur Rubinstein and opera singer Marian Anderson to popular performers such as Nat King Cole, Billy Eckstine, and Cab Calloway(a truly remarkable achievement.

After my encounter with Lloyd Price, I began hanging out at some of the Kingston theaters. On many occasions I would be chased away by Stephen Hill himself, whom I admired from a distance and secretly tried to emulate. But he would always shoo me away, calling me a "dirty little hanger-on."

My waterfront hustling skills, however, soon came in handy. One day while hanging around the Ward and other show spots such as the Carib Theater and the Regal and Tropical Cinemas in Cross Roads, I began to hear complaints from managers that they could not get their performers' stage clothes properly cleaned.

Sensing an opportunity, I immediately began checking out the clothes cleaning scene. After spending one whole week visiting the dry cleaners in Kingston, I decided to offer a professional valet service for artistes visiting Jamaica.

I began keeping track of the comings and goings of all visiting artistes, deciding that I would directly hustle arriving managers for their valet business. Doing so would enable me to cut out the middleman and would specifically bypass Mr. Hill, who I was sure would try to block me.

In no time I had built my valet service into a kind of full-scale personal service for the artistes. In addition to the valet service I began to run errands and to pick up any incidentals the artistes needed. I saw to it that the performers appeared on stage on time in their professionally cleaned performing clothes. Soon my services also included protecting the valuables of visiting performers from thieves. I did this business despite the objections and much to the continued annoyance of Stephen Hill.

Even in those early days, I earned the respect of the people I dealt with, whether it was the businessman whose car I washed, the sailor I showed around Kingston, the lawyer, the trickster, the whore, or the street person; respect given, respect returned became the hallmark of my associations.

My valet and personal service thrived overnight. I boasted such illustrious clients as Fats Domino, Ben E. King, Chuck Jackson (whom I would later manage), and Little Anthony and the Imperials. With time my prestigious list grew to include Patti LaBelle and the Blue Belles and Jerry Butler. All these artistes have expressed their appreciation to me for my professionalism, whether I acted as their Jamaican valet or, in some instances later on, as their manager.

It was also through my valet service that in 1959 I got my first chance to travel.

During my valeting for Little Anthony and the Imperials, I struck up a relationship with a friend of theirs, Phillip Bowe, who had come over from Nassau and who offered basically the same service in the Bahamas as I did in Jamaica. It was not surprising then that after the visit of the Imperials ended, Phillip invited me to visit the Bahamas.

Arriving in Nassau, sixteen years old and with some ten US dollars in my pocket, I began to hang out at such clubs as Jonkanoo and Black Beard's Tavern, which I felt were logical places to practice my valet service to the stars. I was also hoping to find some talent to manage, which was now my ambition.

I began to make friends with most of the entertainers, including such persons as Richie Delmore and the Kemp Brothers, Jonathan and David. It was David Kemp who put me up in a wooden house he owned on Taylor Street which he used intermittently as a meeting spot for his girlfriends. He also got me a job as a bus boy at the Dolphin Hotel, enabling me to survive

My life in Nassau was a stark contrast to my life in Jamaica and prepared me for my US days.

Nassau was then blatantly racist, with most if not all of the black Bahamians confined to over the hill. All the posh stores on Bay Street were owned by white Bahamians, a scenario that eventually led to black consciousness and the long reign of Sir Lynden Pindling and the PLP. To black Bahamians only menial or service jobs were available. Even if you were a born Bahamian, as a black you were still required to identify yourself to security if you were found on the Cable Beach or the tourist side of the island after dark.

Odd as it may seem, because of the nature of the music business, the transition from valet to manager was only one short step. People like me, by the very nature of our exposure to established stars, attracted the interest of newer talent seeking to break into the business. Soon and with great success, I was able to take on the management of the Bahamian calypso singers Tony Seymour and Rusty.

Still, I felt increasingly uncomfortable in Nassau. I was becoming aware that if ever I was to obtain a Bahamian work permit, I had to play my cards cautiously. In the breeze was the ever-present fear Bahamians had of being overrun by the increasing flow of Jamaicans. I found myself always looking over my shoulder and watching my back even though I was also growing quickly in experience in the entertainment business and adding confidence to my management style.

Four to five months after I first arrived in Nassau, I got wind that the Bahamian Immigration was looking for me. I needed no other excuse. I immediately packed what little I had and headed back to Jamaica.

But I returned with my eyes freshly opened and with the resolve to make entertainment management my career.

As it turned out, Bahamian Immigration had done me a favor because I returned to Jamaica just as Jackie Wilson was visiting. I immediately approached him to become his valet and provided him with such excellent service that he offered to buy me a ticket to the USA—Miami to be exact.

After that things moved very quickly. Jackie gave me sixty US dollars for my air ticket and asked me to join him in the USA. But now I needed a visa. It was then that I remembered this military attaché from my hustling days, who worked at the US Embassy located on Duke Street, and who often would visit the downtown bars after hours. I recalled that he had promised me that if I ever got a ticket, he would grant me a visa.

I immediately went to Mr. Chatani who owned a shop located on Harbour Street known as the East Indian Bazaar for a letter of recommendation. In the old days, I used to bring sailors to his shop in exchange for a commission. Without any hesitation, he gave me the recommendation letter, which I hurriedly took to the attaché along with my airplane ticket. That very same day the entry visa was stamped in my passport. Bursting with glee and excitement, I headed straight for 10 Kensington Road, a well-known whorehouse and club owned and run by a friend, Billy Farnum, where I had hung out ever since my return from Nassau.

Billy was a slick, slim, sharp, tall brown Jamaican. His club, the High Hat, and his racehorse, Sir Alec, gave him an aura of flair and style. He would cruise around Kingston in his white Cadillac visiting such friends as Freddie Chin, who owned the Club Havana, where Carlos Malcolm and his Afro-Caribbean music—forerunners of the ska music of the sixties—held sway.

I blurted out to Billy that I was leaving that day with Jackie, and as if by magic, the word spread through the house and, indeed, through the neighborhood: "Don T" was on his way to the USA, and leaving with Jackie Wilson, no less.

Dumping my limited possessions into one small bag, and with a certain sense of importance, amid cheers and best wishes, I jumped into Billy's car and waved good-bye to my friends and neighbors.

It was 1960. I was seventeen years old and excited by the prospect of a new life. My dream of reaching the USA was only a few hours away. For the time being, I was washing my hands of Jamaica. I was ready to plunge into a brand new decade—the sixties.

2

BOB'S EARLY LIFE—
CONCRETE JUNGLE VERSION

The Jamaica I left behind in the fifties was not the land to which I later returned. It was not the Jamaica that Bob Marley was experiencing through the fifties and into the sixties. The rot had set in: the major flood of migration from village to town had begun and the city, especially in the west, had deteriorated.

My side of Kingston, the east side, had always seemed to me a place of gentle breeding and courtesy. We lived there tolerant of each other and aware of common needs. For in those days, perhaps because of colonialism or the advent of self-government, we seemed much more aware of the need to live in harmony. Not for me, then, the violent, divided city, riven by politics and poverty that separated us by crime and violence in armed camps.

In my time, on my side of town, we would walk the streets and acknowledge our neighbor with a smile and a greeting. House doors would remain unlocked. Church doors stayed open. No matter what your station in life, there was a certain civility that transcended class. The city was yours to roam from east to west, from north to south, from one bar to another, from one cinema to the next, whether the Majestic in the west or the Rialto in the east.

The nights as always were noisy, resounding with the barking of dogs, early-morning hours punctuated by the clip-clopping of the horse-drawn carts delivering milk and bread door-to-door. In the background sang the ever-present whistling toads. Evening was heralded by the shrill whistle of the peanut vendor's pushcart. This was Jamaica in the fifties.

But change was in the air. Looking for work, the rural poor had flooded into Kingston, swelling the ranks of the unemployable. The city, unable to absorb or to house them, had deteriorated into rotten pockets of ghettos that festered cheek-by-jowl beside affluent residences. Bob sang about the hurt of this dispossessed horde of newcomers:

> Cold ground was my bed last night
> And rock was my pillow too
> ("Talkin' Blues")

The middle class and the well-to-do had begun to abandon Jones Pen and Trench Town in the west, and Franklin Town and Vineyard Town in the east. New middle-class neighborhoods sprang up in such outlying areas as Mona. In the locally renowned Beverly Hills, concrete mansions towered pretentiously over nearby ghettos.

In addition to these developments, the years since my departure had seen the worldwide decline of colonialism, with Jamaica rapidly moving towards Independence.

In my youthful days of hustling to make a living in Jamaica, I had been unaware of the underlying political and social tensions between people. Years later, I would always find it interesting to compare notes with Bob about our parallel lifestyles, about growing up in different parts of Jamaica during the same period. For while I was living the pain, pleasure and anguish of the Jamaican city boy, Bob Marley, also the descendant of a white man, was growing up first in the hills of St. Ann and then on the other side of the city, in West Kingston.

Whereas I knew my father and could actually approach him on his sober days, Bob never knew his. He, too, had been virtually abandoned by his mother, Cedella, who left him to be raised by his Granny Yaya and his grandfather, Omeriah.

Bob's father, Norval, being a descendant of a supposedly respectable white Jamaican family, would not have been allowed by the social mores of the time to acknowledge his bastard child by a black country woman. The only contact Bob ever had with the Marley family, he told me, was when he visited his uncle, a lawyer on Duke Street, and tried to borrow £300 to produce a record. The uncle, one Cecil Marley, not only unceremoniously threw Bob out of his office, he also called the police.

A rural child, Bob was raised in the hills of Nine Miles in St. Ann where his grandfather, a farmer, lived a typical Jamaican peasant's life full of hardship, but spiced with Anancy stories, folk riddles, Blackheart tales and wise African proverbs. His grandparents were able to trace their ancestry from the Coromantee slaves of the tribe of Akan, a tribe noted both for its resilience and prophetic powers.

Abandoned by his mother at an early age when she moved to Spanish Town to live with a Chinese man, Bob attended Stepney School in St. Ann. He often told me that he would never forget the day he had been sent by Granny to visit his mother at her shop. When he walked into the shop and called her, "Mama," she brusquely challenged him, "Who yu a call Mama?" This incident left an indelible mark on him, and it was a story he often told.

In speaking of his early life Bob always emphasized that he had grown up feeling closest to Granny. She saw to his every need as a child in Nine Miles, St. Ann, a parish historically steeped in the ways of the plantocracy. For example, Brown's Town, one of St. Ann's main towns, boasted one of the island's best upper-class girls' schools, St. Hilda's, which literally lived up to the town's name by never admitting black girls. Bob himself had the right tint to fit into the plantocracy, but he lacked the right upbringing.

Like many other rural boys, Bob soon realized that St. Ann held nothing for him. Encouraged by his "cousin" Bunny Livingston, later known as Bunny Wailer (with whom he shared an early interest in music), Bob made up his mind to move to Kingston where his mother was now living with Bunny's father, Thaddeus, in Trench Town.

Trench Town and the rest of West Kingston had by then become large tracts of wasteland crammed with the makeshift houses of the itinerant rural squatters who had captured every square inch of living space. Its festering shacks were built cheek-by-jowl. Unaccountably the politicians thought that the way to solve the problem of ghetto rot was simply to bulldoze the hovels and replace them with large concrete structures such as Rema and Tivoli. In Kingston, Bob ended up in one of these neighborhoods that the country would later call "Concrete Jungle."

It was here that Bob began his association with Peter Tosh. Bunny had already joined him, and their interest in music brought the three together.

Then and now, young ghetto dwellers typically spent many idle days without regular work or opportunities. It was a world whose only escape seemed to be for boys to learn a trade or for girls to clean the houses of the rich, or for the entire family to migrate to "foreign," usually with the mother leaving first and the family following later. For recreation, ghetto boys played cards, dominoes and had early sexual experiences. Any girl who had not borne a child by fifteen was regarded contemptuously as a mule.

The only relief from idleness and tension were the blues dances featuring the sound systems of Sir Coxsone Downbeat held at Love Lane and Beeston Street and at Cho Co Mo Lawn. Here sharply dressed youth would gyrate to the beat of Fats Domino and Louis Jordan and his Tympany Five, while blissfully inhaling the ganja that heightened their appreciation of the local kings of toasting such as King Sporty, King Stitt and Count Machub, the real forerunners of Dee Jaying, rapping and hip hop.

The only other escape was the creative talent of the individual, and with the increasing availability of the transistor radio, thousands of which were now in Jamaica, the world of music soon began to attract the sufferers and dreamers who lived in the ghettos. Bob was one of those who found music irresistible.

In this era of his life, it was to Vincent "Tata" Ford that Bob told me he turned for guidance and comfort and with whom he virtually lived. He slept in Tata's kitchen, where he met Rita and consummated their relationship.

Over the years Bob continually expressed to me his deep love, appreciation and trust of Tata Ford, whose name he subsequently used as the writer of "No Woman No Cry," a song set in Tata's government yard that spoke of people Bob actually knew.

> I remember when we used to sit
> In a government yard in Trench Town.

Trench Town was crammed with stark concrete structures and a network of unpaved footpaths, with few trees and little or no grass. Human waste was disposed of in open pits. The night was lit by the flickering glow of kerosene lanterns and kitchen bitches. Running water was available only in the government tenement yards or through the odd standpipe. Thank God for the transistor radio which needed no electricity, and allowed an escape to the wide world of music.

As Bob said in 1975, "We used to sing in the back of Trench Town and rehearse plenty until the Drifters came 'pon the scene, and mi group singing, so me just say, well me 'ave fe go look a group."

Now that Bob was living near his mother, Cedella, who had by this time become very church conscious, he was finding it increasingly difficult to deal with her. She was constantly pushing him to learn a trade as a way out of the ghetto. Bob finally agreed to enroll in school and learn welding. But he was far more interested in the music and attracted to the Rastafarian religion, which was becoming increasingly popular in Trench Town. Bob was intrigued by Rastafarianism's haughty rejection of the material world and the injustices heaped on the people by "Babylon," or the establishment. His differences with his mother increased, especially as he seemed to be becoming, in her eyes, an admirer of the rude boy culture that was beginning to impact on Jamaican society.

In the ghetto world the motto was dog eat dog, kill or be killed. For survival, it was necessary to fight in defense of one's territory and rights. With the divisions between Laborite community and PNP camps widening, political grouping became increasingly important. The emerging rude boy culture echoed a new aggression and divisiveness.

Now the fire is burning...
Ride natty ride
Go deh dready, go deh
("Ride Natty Ride")

Their hopes and frustrations mirrored in the music that reflected the rude boy image of the time, the ghetto youth fiercely defended their home turfs. Political culture and partisanship grew and became more and more bitter throughout the Concrete Jungle. Sound system music and the Rastafarian religion competed as other important influences. The music world expanded and exploded, embracing Count P, Duke Reid and his Treasure Isle label and Clement Dodd, a cabinet maker turned DJ who hired Prince Buster and selector Lee Perry to expand the impact of his sound system.

Coxsone's Musik City opened in 1959. Here Bob spent many hours and eventually got up enough courage to show his songs to Dodd. But as fate would have it, he ran, instead, into Leslie Kong at Federal Records, for whom he recorded his first-ever songs, "Judge Not" and "Do You Still Love Me," for twenty pounds.

Meanwhile it was to Mortimer Planno of the Divine Theocratic Temple to whom Bob turned for guidance and explanation of the Rastafarian religion.

Planno taught Bob about the stages of Rastafarianism, taking him to the settlements deep in the interior of the country where he learned about the grounation ceremonies, and the all-night convocations of feasting on coconut meat, rice and peas (ital cooking). It was here that he listened to the traditional Bongo Man and the Humba and Nyabinghi chants, while hundreds of Rastas sat on their haunches passing the sacred chillum pipe.

The Rasta women would sit apart from the men, especially if they were menstruating—a state Rastas regard as unclean. In the Rasta religion women have a restricted role. They can't wear make-up and perfumes. They are required to always dress modesty.

During this learning time with Planno, Bob's spirituality manifested itself in a dream.

In his dream an old man attired in khaki appeared to Bob as an emissary of the deceased Norval Marley (Bob's father) and presented Bob with a curious black jeweled ring. Bob told Planno that on telling his mother of this dream, she had produced the very ring in the dream and slipped it on Bob's finger. Wearing it, Bob confided, had made him extremely uncomfortable. Planno interpreted the dream to mean that Bob would either grow in spirituality through his experiences or he would "Ketch a fire" (catch hell)—which would later be the name of one of Bob's albums.

Welding, Bob's grudgingly accepted trade, did not hold him for long, and soon a steel sliver in his eye forced him to quit. This accident, however, only heightened the tension between Bob and his mother. Objecting strongly to his Rastafarian leanings and his smoking of ganja, she virtually banned him from her home. He ended up sleeping in Tata's kitchen.

In later years, Bob would lose some respect for his mother when, in the face of his rising worldwide recognition, she adopted his Rasta faith. To see her come full circle, smoking the weed and calling him Brother Bob, never sat comfortably with him, and on one occasion during a discussion of some personal business, he sarcastically remarked, "Don Taylor, you don't know my mother."

Following his recording of some five more songs including "One Cup of Coffee," Bob, whose musical strength and confidence were already showing, had broken with Kong. His group had by now become known as the Wailers and was complete with the addition of two Rema girls to sing backup and Junior Braithwaite to share the vocals.

Somewhere around this time the first Wailers album, *Simmer Down*, done with Coxsone Dodd, was released.

Meanwhile, the political climate in Jamaica was heating up. Norman Manley's PNP government had lost a critical referendum intended to unite Jamaica and the other Caribbean islands in a Federation. On the heels of this defeat, the JLP government of Alexander Bustamante had swept into office, taking the country into Independence on August 3, 1962.

Independence intensified the hopes and aspirations of the people, who fervently believed that their sad lives would change with the new era. The celebrations and euphoria sweeping the island further aggravated the situation. Thousands of the poor drifted into the city, hungry for rumored opportunities.

West Kingston, from which the musical Marley was emerging, had always been the center both of culture and violent political swings. Its ghetto music offered solace to the suffering poor:

> One good thing about music
> When it hits you, you feel no pain.
> ("Trench Town Rock")

By coincidence the political representative of the West was Edward Seaga, who was himself steeped in Jamaican music and would become the first record producer on the WIRL (West Indies Recording Limited) label, forming part of the original small body of producers that included Leslie Kong, Coxsone Dodd and Duke Reid.

A Harvard-trained anthropologist, Seaga, after receiving his degree in 1952, had proceeded to study the history and development of revivalist cults and the indigenous music forms of Kumina, Pocomania, and Obeah practices in Jamaica. In 1955, during his pre-political days, Seaga released an album of cult music on the Ethnic Folkways label and set out to develop in the ghettos of West Kingston an opportunity through music that its residents had long awaited.

Seaga moved the music into more commercial territory and from his base in Cho Co Mo Lawn began to record sessions at JBC and Federal Records. He signed such Trench Town or West Kingston groups as Joe Higgs and Roy-Wilson to the WIRL label. Out of this came the Higgs and Wilson 1959 ska track, "Manny O," which sold an unprecedented thirty thousand copies. Even more startling, for the first time a producer made sure that the artiste was actually paid. Seaga then went on to sign up such additional talent as Slim Smith and Byron Lee.

Joe Higgs, himself long influenced by the Rasta faith, now brought his influence to bear on ghetto music by starting a music clinic in Rema. Using his knowledge and skill and access to the records of such stars as Nat King Cole, Billy Eckstine and Lord Kitchener, he taught his pupils—among them Bob Marley, Bunny Wailer and Peter Tosh—the rudiments of music.

Around this time Bob also met up with Danny Sims and Johnny Nash and the whole story which has become linked to Cayman Music and Sims Publishing Company was born.

It was shortly after Bunny Wailer was sent to prison for smoking ganja that Bob, having returned to St. Ann, was approached by Johnny Nash, his personal manager Danny Sims, and Arthur Jenkins, all of whom were visiting Jamaica.

They persuaded Marley to sign to the US JAD (Johnny, Arthur and Danny) label.

Johnny Nash subsequently paid for Bob to go to Europe to make an album, and appear in a film scene. In the end, the album became only one single, and the scene was never shot.

Johnny Nash, however, struck gold with his cover version "Guava Jelly," coming out of his *I Can See Clearly Now* album.

Bob complained about not being paid what he was due, and said, "Me don't want to say nothing bad 'bout them, but still me no have nothin' much good to say." He had learned a bitter lesson.

All that time, Bob was also recording with the Wailers for Lee Perry, producing such tracks as "Soul Rebel," "It's All Right," and "Duppy Conqueror." Working with Lee Perry on these songs, I would later learn, taught Bob all he knew about laying music. When I was producing Martha Valez's "Disco Nights"—written by Bob for Sire Records, the independent arm of Time/ Warner—Bob hired Lee Perry to work with him. I recall Bob saying that no one was better than Lee "Scratch" Perry at laying rhythms. We did the recording at Harry J's studios.

During this period, the political mood was turning uglier. Arnett Gardens was bulldozed by the PNP politicians to make way for a new development. Political divisions and tensions intensified as old residents were pushed out by PNP supporters brought in to create a new constituency. Concrete Jungle was created. Meanwhile, *Soul Revolution*, the second Wailers album, was igniting the charts.

The studios of Perry and Kong were releasing the Wailers' tunes, but not to the liking of Bunny, Peter and Bob. The disgruntled Wailers, who knew they were being exploited, put a curse on Leslie Kong. Shortly afterwards, Kong dropped dead at thirty-eight of a heart attack. Kong had had no previous history of heart trouble. The story of Bob's deadly curse, coupled with Planno's interpretation of the dream and the ring, made the rounds, creating the aura of mysticism that would surround Bob all his life.

The political temperature kept rising, continuously fueled by the sounds of the ghetto. Because many of the stars in the ska scene were Rastas, a national rude boy identity began to emerge out of the music.

Seaga had by now forsaken the musical world for politics and, using his knowledge of ghetto life, delivered a major political speech as senator about *the haves* and *the have nots*. In 1954, Bustamante had appointed him to the Senate as minister of development and welfare.

The early divisiveness of the political scene with its two-party rivalries had continued to worsen, with Seaga charging that the police were hired guns for the PNP and Manley accusing Seaga of thuggery. The stage for future bloody confrontation had been set. Many would, indeed, marvel at the audacity of Seaga, a white Lebanese Jamaican, for trying to carve out a stake in the black-controlled ghettos of the west, and even winning a seat in the 1962 elections against none other than the "Burning Spear," Dudley Thompson, who had just returned from Africa after defending Jomo Kenyatta.

The political turmoil became too much for Bob's mother. She left for the USA and settled in Delaware. She could never understand Bob's love for the ghetto and his unusual approach to life. To explain how he felt, Bob would often repeat Granny's famous saying, "When the root is strong, the fruit is sweet."

With his mother gone, Bob plunged deeper into the music world. And as new studios opened and opportunities increased, so did the impact of his music. Yet his music and the music of the ghetto still had not gained acceptance from the upper-class Jamaicans, who saw it as an insult to their culture.

One person who loved ghetto music was the innovative and creative Byron Lee, a Jamaican of Chinese descent, who had himself now joined the ranks of record producers, having acquired Seaga's WIRL label and worked out a deal with Atlantic Records to launch ska commercially. His entry into the business coincided with Millie Small's 1964 world hit, "My Boy Lollipop" following her arrival in England where she recorded it on the Island label owned by one Chris Blackwell. Offspring of the plantocracy, Blackwell had discovered a niche from which he could make big money.

The music itself was changing from ska to rock steady and had begun to produce such major successes as Blues Busters, Millie Small, Desmond Dekker and the Aces. The music world began to take note.

Not surprisingly it was Seaga who capitalized on the new craze and decided as minister of development and welfare to send a ska delegation to the 1964 New York World's Fair to exploit for tourism the potential of this emerging Jamaican music. That year he also earned the respect of the Rastafarians by bringing Marcus Garvey's body back to Jamaica.

Back on the home front, with the sound systems growing in appeal and intensity, Coxsone asked Bob to develop material for the Soulettes, Rita Marley's group.

Born in Cuba, Rita had been brought to Jamaica as an infant by her parents, who subsequently left her behind as they migrated to England. She knew her father, Roy Anderson, was somewhere in Europe. Rita, who was then nineteen, had been raised by her strict and demanding Auntie Viola, and had already borne a child, Sharon.

Bob never really liked Auntie and would always say that she was a practitioner of obeah (Jamaican voodoo). He told me he was afraid of her. His relationship with Rita, however, developed in spite of Auntie, and they ended up living together and producing some four children during this period.

Bob's mother Cedella never stopped trying to bring him to the USA, but he refused to go, showing little or no desire to leave the ghetto, where by now he had earned the reputation of "Gong," a descriptive word for the toughest.

The island's continuing economic problems, however, had not eased but worsened, heightening the attraction of the rude boy culture and its appeal to the neglected masses. Independence had not brought prosperity but only harsher poverty. Cedella continued to plead with Bob to come to the USA, finally wearing him down with the argument that his migration would help his children find a better life. In 1965 Bob at last agreed to join his mother in Delaware. To make it easier for his children to get their own visas, he married Rita.

From the start Bob never liked America and missed Jamaica. In his absence, the local music business was growing to the point that Jamaican acts were opening for such visiting stars as Betty Everett and Ben E. King. For the rest of his life Bob was always bitter that his sojourn in the USA also caused him to miss the visit to Jamaica of the Emperor, His Imperial Majesty Haile Selassie, who arrived at Palisadoes Airport on April 21, 1966. Bob had wanted very much wanted to be a part of that climactic event but had to settle for hearing about it secondhand from Rita.

This visit saw a throng of some 100,000 people turn up at the airport, exceeding even the wildest expectations. At the request of the officials, Mortimer Planno had to quiet the crowd so that His Majesty could deplane.

Bob's stay in America was short lived. When Rita joined him in August 1966 with her daughter, Sharon, Bob promptly sent her back. And shortly afterwards, when he lost his job and learned that he was eligible to be drafted into the US Army, he left the USA and returned to where he knew he really belonged—Jamaica.

3

MAKING IT IN THE
LAND OF OPPORTUNITY
— USA VERSION

Unlike Bob's short sojourn with his mother in the USA, my escape to the good life took me to the gateway of music. On my arrival, I picked up on the contacts I had made in the Bahamas and Jamaica. One of the first people I got in touch with was Dizzy Jones.

I had met Dizzy Jones and his group—consisting of two guys called Sam and Dave—after they had been stranded in Jamaica by Stephen Hill following a failed concert. They had been staying at Mrs. Enid Bruce's guesthouse, where Hill lodged his second-rate stars.

Sam and Dave were trying to earn enough money to pay their fare back to Miami. In my first booking anywhere, I contacted Freddie Chin, who, like his friend Billy Farnum, drove a big white fishtail Cadillac and staged a lot of foreign shows, though his main occupation was to bring in female dancers from the Dominican Republic. One evening I took Sam, Dave and Dizzy to the Club Havana to meet Freddie, who hired them for a week so that they could earn their fare back home. Sam, Dave, Dizzy and I became close, and they told me that if I ever got to Miami, they would repay the favor.

On my arrival in Miami, I headed straight for the hotel off 7th Avenue where they lived. Miami was then still fairly segregated, with its black population herded into the overtown area.

The hotel was an all-night hangout for hustlers, party people, drinkers and prostitutes. Its rooms came in three prices: eight dollars with the bathroom down the hall, ten dollars with toilet and no shower, and fifteen dollars for a room with toilet and shower. The hotel was owned by a light-brown blind man whose family was rich and involved in politics.

It was at this same hotel that one of Miami's biggest disc jockeys, Butter Ball, lived. A Miami legend, Butler worked at radio station WMBM, which was number-one station in Miami, and often hosted a cookout for kids.

One block from the hotel, right in the middle of a black neighborhood, was the number-one club in Miami, the white-owned Sir John's Nite Beat. A couple of blocks away was the Cargo Hotel which, with the Nite Beat Club, formed the core of the exciting Miami nightlife.

Dizzy, Sam or Dave were all happy to see me when we finally met the next morning. Dizzy asked what I would be doing, and I told him I was here to try to make it. He offered me a night job waiting tables at his club in Liberty City. After that meeting, I went and had breakfast—eggs, grits and coffee for thirty-nine cents.

The first week of waiting tables at Dizzy's club, I earned sixty dollars plus about eight dollars a night in tips. After paying rent, I had sixty-five dollars left in my pocket. A few days later I met a girl, and we went about a lot together. One day, claiming to have forgotten her purse at home, she asked me to lend her forty dollars. I did and never saw her or my money again. I record the incident here for posterity to show that

Don Taylor, super-hustler, was himself once hustled. I found out later she was a heroin addict.

To make ends meet, I realized that I had to find something to do during the days. I went to the employment agency and got a few days' work at a bagel bakery. The following week, I was sent to Denny's Restaurant on the beach to wash dishes for one dollar and forty cents per hour, then the minimum wage.

On my way to work at Denny's one day, I had my first brush with American racism.

The bus I had boarded for the ride to the beach suddenly stopped at the police station next to the bridge. The driver ordered, "All Negroes and colored people off the bus." I later learned that there was a pass system in effect requiring black people to check in with the police. You had to tell the police where you were going, why, and how long your business would take. If you were caught on the beach after the stated time, you would be arrested for loitering with intent to steal.

During my third week in Miami, I met Dominic Schiffoni, Jackie Wilson's manager, who had toured with him in Jamaica. He used his influence to get me a job carrying bags at the Miami Beach Crown Hotel.

A week later, fortune smiled on me again. Jerry Butler came to the Sir John's Nite Beat Club to work for the weekend and, upon seeing me again, immediately offered me forty dollars a week plus room and board to join his tour as his valet.

This innocent meeting turned out to be the beginning of my entry into show business in the United States and the consequent tremendous success that I have achieved today.

We departed Miami a few days later, bound for Tampa, Florida, where we stayed at the Sheraton Hotel. The following morning I ventured out on the road looking for something to eat. Because I was not very familiar with American food, I stuck mostly to eating hamburgers or tuna fish sandwiches. When I entered this restaurant to order tuna fish on toast, the man behind the counter barked my order out as one tuna fish to go. Politely and innocently I explained to him that I intended to eat my sandwich here. Handing me my sandwich in a paper bag, he said, "Boy, don't you know we don't allow niggers to eat in our restaurant?"

Jerry worked his way up to the next city in Florida, Jacksonville, which had a much larger black population and where we were to meet up with another tour starting there and including Sam Cooke, Chuck Jackson, the Drifters, the Shirelles, Patti LaBelle and the Blue Belles and a host of unknowns such as Gladys Knight and the Pips.

The tour was being promoted by Henry Wynn, an extraordinary black man whom I consider to be a legend. He represented what I thought I wanted to be at that time, if for no other reason than that he was everything to everybody. He owned a liquor store on Auburn Avenue in Atlanta. He had an interest in the Forest Arms Hotel—the only hotel blacks could stay in at that time. He was also the number-one numbers man in Atlanta.

His Auburn Avenue clubs drew a growing crowd of black consciousness leaders, including such stellar personalities as Martin Luther King, Andrew Young and Jesse Jackson, and contributed to the sweet Auburn Avenue myth.

Henry Wynn was single-handedly responsible for the growth of black music and black companies such as Motown. He was the first person to have the vision to take a group of acts on a bus tour of the USA. Initially, because most of the acts were black, this move was greeted with hostility. Later Dick Clark used the same idea after watering it down with a mixture of mainly white plus a few black acts. His touring acts met with great success by appealing to the white audiences and became the start of Clark's empire. In contrast, Henry Wynn ended up dying in jail for tax evasion, for no other reason than because he was a black man in a white-controlled world.

The tour with Jerry Butler lasted thirty days and allowed me to see a part of American life, especially in the South, that I had never imagined possible. I witnessed behavior by white people that I could not have predicted, never having seen that side of them in Jamaica. Many a time we were refused lodgings in spite of having made reservations, simply because we were black. We would arrive at auditoriums and not be allowed to perform because we were black. In some auditoriums, blacks and whites sat separated by chicken wire.

The experience I obtained from this tour, by my exposure to these future greats as well as to the management style of Henry Wynn and others, added to my later development as a successful manager. I did not miss the opportunity to watch and learn.

With the tour at an end, Jerry returned to Chicago, his home town, taking me along with him. We had two weeks between tours, and Jerry used the time to move into a new townhouse which he had just purchased and which, to this day, he still occupies. I stayed at a nearby hotel.

During the next two weeks, I helped Jerry move into his house and get ready for our next stop, which was to be New York City at the famed Apollo Theater, a stopover I looked forward to with great excitement. Jerry and I rode his Cadillac El Dorado from Chicago to New York. He alone did the driving. The one time he had allowed me to drive, I drifted over to the left, the side we drive on in Jamaica, and was spared a collision only because he woke up, grabbed the wheel, and steered us to safety. He never trusted my driving again.

We arrived in New York and checked into the Gorham Hotel on 55th Street between 6th and 7th Avenue, where we stayed for the duration of the performances. But during that week at the Apollo, I got into an argument with Jerry's percussionist and bandleader Jamo Thomas, about what I can't remember. Jamo, who was more important to the band than I was, demanded my dismissal, leaving Jerry no choice. I was fired and left behind in New York.

The experience made me swear to become more important, indispensable even, in all my future roles in music.

Although I had only just arrived in New York, I had already met many show business people, including the charming Tammi Montgomery. The city and the music scene, however, still struck me as a jungle of confusion.

After a few days of battering around New York, I called a friend of Jerry B's, Charles McMillan, a schoolteacher in a small town in Pennsylvania, and he invited me to stay with him and his mother in Chesterville, a seaport town so much like Kingston that I immediately felt at home. I made friends quickly with assorted pimps, hustlers and prostitutes, not unlike the street people I had known in Jamaica.

During my four-month stay in Chesterville, I kept in close contact with Tammi, who would later become famous as Tammi Terrell. Tammi was being managed then by the young heirs to the Gimbels Department Store who, at her request, gave me a job as a stock boy for a salary of forty-two US dollars in the Gimbels Germantown store. It was during one of my treks from Chesterville to Germantown that I saw posters advertising an upcoming show at the Uptown Theater featuring Little Anthony and the Imperials with Joe Tex, the Supremes, and the Temptations.

Anxious to return to show business, I contacted Little Anthony and got back the valet job I had had some two years before when they were in the Bahamas with the now famous Hubert Laws. The tour was a success, culminating with a final performance in Brooklyn, New York, where the Imperials were born and raised.

After the tour, with my job with the Imperials only requiring three or fours days per week of work, I began roaming the streets of Brooklyn and learning street games. I briefly hustled numbers, in a game similar to "drop pan" in Jamaica, using my earnings to fund poker games called rent parties because the players all used their winnings to pay rent. Life in Brooklyn on the streets, I found, was no different than street life on Kingston's waterfront: everyone hustled to survived.

During this time I began to worry about my immigrant status. I had been in the US now for some four to five years illegally. Sooner or later I would be caught and sent back to Jamaica. There were only two options open to me that might make my stay legal: one was to get an a honorable discharge from the military; the other was to marry a US citizen. The first option seemed unlikely, since joining the military required either resident immigrant status or US citizenship. I explained my dilemma to a friend I'll call Myles, and he advised me to go to some country town and register for the draft. He suggested that when I registered, I act dumb and claim that my father had been a US sailor. With the Vietnam war raging, he said, the authorities were unlikely to check up on my story.

I took his advice and it worked. In August 1965 I received a letter from the draft board ordering me to report for US military service in Philadelphia at 9:00 a.m. on October 25, 1965.

After doing basic training at Fort Jackson, South Carolina, Fort Benning, Georgia, and attending airborne school, I was stationed in Fort Ord, California, for the remainder of my tour of duty, assigned to the Special Services Branch, the office responsible for providing entertainment to the armed forces.

For two years, the army became the mother and father I had never had. For the first time in my life, I was under caring supervision, fed three meals a day, given clothes to wear, and treated to free dental care and every other perk that middle-class children take for granted as a birthright. I was twenty-one years old before I inherited all these blessings.

When I had been an urchin roaming the waterfront, I used to quietly ask God why was I so "bad lucky" as to have been born in Jamaica and not in the USA, why I, too, couldn't have been a passenger aboard one of those luxurious ocean liners that used to sail in and out of Kingston harbor. Now I was an American citizen. And the army had given Don Taylor, US 52-652-558, the necessary discipline and self-respect to successfully travel the road of life.

During my two years' stint in the army, I made sure to stay in touch with show business. Whenever possible, while on leave, I would make trips with groups like the Drifters.

On my discharge from the US Army on October 25, 1967, I immediately headed for New York City. There, I charted the course which would enable me to renew my acquaintance with people such as Chuck Jackson and Little Anthony and the Imperials, this time, however, as their manager, not their valet.

How I became the manager of Little Anthony and the Imperials is a kind of storybook dream.

The Imperials were then the clients of the William Morris booking agency, then run by Lee Solomon who had himself discovered Peggy Lee, and who had the power to affect the career of black performers seeking to cross over to the white charts.

The group was appearing at the Newport Beach Hotel in Miami, when a difference developed between the Imperials and the agency. Phil Strasberg, manager of the Imperials, was pushed by the Imperials to ask for a meeting with Lee Solomon to discuss the problem. I myself was the road manager at the time. It seemed obvious to me that Phil did not want to call the meeting, that he had little confidence in his ability to speak for the group and solve its problem.

On the day of the meeting, he made his insecurity even more obvious by first sitting on the ledge beside Lee Solomon instead of on our side of the table, and by opening the meeting with the remark, "Well, we are here because the boys have a problem."

I could immediately feel a charge run through all of us, and when I saw Sammy Strain—one of the Imperials—glare at Lee, I knew the matter would not end there.

As soon as we left the meeting and were headed downstairs Sammy told Phil he was fired. When Phil recovered and asked why, a thunder of voices brought home to him the simple truth that as their manager, the Imperials expected their problem to be his problem, too.

With Phil gone, I took over the duties of the group's manager while we searched for a replacement. One candidate we contacted was J. W. Alexander, who was then also managing Sam Cooke and Lou Rawls. He came and listened to the group report on their plans and on what they had been doing while I acted as their temporary manager.

When the group had finished, J.W. said, "You guys don't need a manager, you have a manager." To me, he added, "Don, you are a manager, you are their manager." He then turned to them and said, "Give Don the money and the position."

That was how I became the manager of the Imperials. In that role, I met the challenge and actually took the group to new heights with such hits as "Going Out of My Mind" and "Hurt So Bad." When there were no hits, I did what very few managers have done: for twelve years I kept them steadily working Las Vegas.

My experience as a musical group's manager seasoned me in the intricacies of the business. I gained entry into the world of the Mafia, with whom, like all managers, I became closely associated, developing a lasting friendship with many of their members.

Some years later in Las Vegas, I met J.W. again, this time in the company of Colonel Parker, who was with Elvis Presley, the main attraction playing the casinos. I had just returned from Jamaica and was wearing a straw hat. As J. W. was telling Colonel Parker how I had got my start, the Colonel reached over, took off my hat, placed it on his own head and said, "From all I have heard from J.W., you have started a brilliant career and you are going to be big." I never saw that hat again.

Over the years, as our paths crisscrossed in Las Vegas, I developed a good relationship both with Elvis and his manager.

I learned a lot from the Colonel. I admired his shrewdness. He looked after Elvis well and always made sure that his star dressed and that, during the very early days, his concerts were always full—even if the tickets had to be given away!

I liked Elvis a lot, too. To me, he seemed like a real person. Even though he was a mega-star, he never swaggered around playing the part.

One day we were at a house Little Anthony had rented in Las Vegas when, at eight o'clock in the evening, the doorbell rang. I answered it and there was Elvis, with four bodyguards.

He was dressed in a smart jumpsuit, but not the fancy kind he wore on stage.

He came in and he sat on the sofa talking to Little Anthony. We were amused to see that when he got up to go to the bathroom, all four bodyguards automatically got up, followed him, and stood waiting outside the door. Elvis didn't seem to find this behavior odd. We ended up at the Sahara Hotel where the guys ordered something to eat—burgers, I think—for dinner in the dressing room.

Anthony and Elvis were very relaxed with each other and got along well. When they were together, they reminisced about music, about the good old days. Elvis joked about the first time they had met in 1958 on the *Ed Sullivan Show*. He told us that as soon as he started singing the camera moved from his body and stayed riveted to his head.

I respected Elvis—and the Colonel. And when the Colonel predicted that I'd make it big, I knew deep down that my love and respect for the industry would prove his words correct.

Little did I know that marking my mark would involve me with reggae's biggest performer—Bob Marley.

THE MAN

4

MARLEY AND ME —
FIRST ENCOUNTERS

I was at home in Los Angeles one day attending to the business of Little Anthony and the Imperials, when the phone rang. It was Stephen Hill Sr., on a visit to Los Angeles from Jamaica. He asked if I would help him find a singer to do a benefit for the Trench Town Sports Complex in Jamaica. His son had become involved with Member of Parliament Anthony Spaulding and was very keen on the benefit. Hill invited me to the Hyatt House Hotel on Sunset Boulevard where he was staying, to go over names of possible artistes we might ask to perform.

Jamaica now had a new, recently elected prime minister, Michael Manley, with whom I had become quite impressed. Even though I had been abroad for years, Jamaican politics was still in my blood. Ours is an island whose people eat, sleep, and breathe politics.

Manley had begun to speak for the poor and their desperate needs. He was emphasizing the urgency of opening Jamaican society to the formerly disenfranchised. Everything he preached appealed to my inner instincts and related to my own background of desperate struggle and hard-won achievement.

He had appointed to his cabinet people who were known to be sympathetic to the needs and wants of the poor and who offered them hope. One such person was Tony Spaulding, the minister of housing.

I was actually by then passionately committed to Michael Manley and his PNP government. If Manley or Spaulding had asked me to jump, I would have asked "How high?" I later learned that Bob himself felt the same way, having clawed his way with his musical genius out of the brutal jungle of Trench Town, part of Tony Spaulding's constituency.

The approach of Manley's government was in sharp contrast with that of the previous Shearer/JLP government, which had seemed unsympathetic to the rising tide of black consciousness.

In 1967 the black Hugh Shearer had succeeded Sangster as prime minister and leader of the JLP. His government promptly enacted travel bans and immigration restrictions on such persons as Walter Rodney, a Guyanese lecturer at the University of the West Indies and a strong black power advocate, a decision that led to general unrest, demonstrations and rioting. In addition, the Shearer government not only banned various black consciousness books and periodicals, it also sought to suppress the publication of a radical local newspaper, *Abeng*. Even Julian Bond, a respected supporter of the civil rights movement in the USA, was barred from visiting Jamaica without special clearance. Stokely Carmichael and Malcolm X were names that sent tremors through this government.

It was against this background that Michael Manley rose to power.

Now looking back, I realize that Manley was given to flights of rhetoric that went way beyond what he was either willing or able to do. In his mind, rhetoric and myth became entangled with fact and reality. He became absorbed in a cult of his own words. On reflection, Manley's tenure may even have badly skewed the thinking of Jamaica and contributed to the island's problems today.

To my mind, the rhetorical and divisive political approach of Michael Manley during the 1970s produced a backlash condition in Jamaica that, in the nineties, has resulted in a scornful and harsh public attitude towards the poor. It is a legacy not dissimilar to the one spawned by the Reagan/Bush presidencies, which created the highest level of recession in the USA while reintroducing a bitter racism I thought the country had outgrown.

But with Michael Manley in power now for only a year, things had changed dramatically. Rastafarianism had gained respectability and now permeated to the children of the middle and upper classes, who adopted its beliefs in unprecedented numbers. Long gone were the days when Rastas were in danger of having their heads forcibly shaved by the police.

Under the new Manley government, homage was now being openly paid to Mother Africa. Michael Manley himself boasted in speeches that he had been handed a "Rod of Correction" by Haile Selassie, God to all Rastafarians. "Jah Rastafari" became a familiar street cry that took on more and more significance in the evolving cultural and musical expression of the common people.

It was in this context that Stephen Hill Sr., had asked for my help. With my political sympathies, I was quite willing to give it.

I immediately suggested asking Marvin Gaye, with whom I was still in touch, to do the benefit. Hill quickly agreed. I put him in touch with Yvonne Fair, whom I had known from my days of being a valet for Chuck Jackson, and who was now a solo artiste with Motown Records. She deserves every credit for getting Marvin Gaye to perform in Jamaica.

Stephen Hill then asked me if I would pick up the expense of getting Marvin Gaye to Jamaica for the benefit, promising me reimbursement later for the estimated twenty thousand US dollars cost. Because the concert was for a worthy cause, I agreed. But to this day I have never received full reimbursement. I am still out of pocket some ten thousand US dollars.

Way back in the mid-sixties, I had met Marvin when he was a part-time chauffeur for Berry Gordy and struggling to break into show business. With Yvonne's help, it was not difficult to convince him to fly with me to Jamaica to support the government's fund-raising efforts for the depressed areas of Trench Town. Marvin would, in fact, be technically performing free or, in reality, at my expense. The cause was a good one and being a part of it would give me a chance to help the Manley government and its welcome change of emphasis on the needs of the poor.

Marvin having agreed to be the star attraction, I flew with him to the concert to discover that Bob Marley was slated as the opening act.

At the time I did not know much about Marley. I only knew that he had written songs for Barbra Streisand and Eric Clapton and that he had had one major hit with his "I Shot the Sheriff." Bob was then still under contract to Danny Sims and Cayman Music.

During the trip, Marvin was struck by the freedom with which Jamaicans and Jamaican performers used ganja. He was floored by the purity and strength of the Jamaican homegrown herb, which Bob used freely and openly. Also during this trip, Stephen Hill and Marvin Gaye hit it off, ending up with Hill eventually becoming Marvin's manager. The rest is history—a history that chronicles the rise and fall of Marvin's career until his sad and untimely death on April 1, 1984, at his own father's hand. He was then still being managed by Stephen Hill.

I remember Marvin with affection as an understanding and generous man. Once, when he was a struggling singer, someone cheated him. Marvin didn't get mad. He simply said, "They can cheat me, but they can't cheat God."

Marvin was a kind man who was, in many ways, his own worst enemy. Not unlike Bob, he shouldered everyone else's burdens as well as his own. He started a company, made his sister its manager, and watched helplessly while she lost millions.

During the trip for the Trench Town benefit, I finally met Marley face to face. Bob and his representative had visited the Sheraton Hotel in New Kingston looking for Stephen Hill to pay them for the concert appearance. Hill, they felt, was giving them the runaround. I advised Hill that this mishandling was no way to treat a performer. Later I was told that Bob was impressed by my straightforwardness. I had spoken up partly because Tony Spaulding had specifically sent Jean Barnes to see that Bob was treated properly.

Later that day I met Bob again. He turned to me and asked, "Yu really is a Jamaican?" I said, "Yes," to which Bob then replied, "How yuh learn the business so?" I told him that I had been in the USA since the days of my youth and had learned the business through hard experience. He said, "Then nuh a man like yuh me a look for, because with a man like yuh around and with your knowledge, when mi chat me nuh have fi repeat miself."

Bob and I swapped intermittent telephone calls for a year after this meeting in 1973, always promising to get together, periodically leaving messages for one another. But the vagaries of the music business, and my own sometimes bad habit of not returning calls, caused us to miss making a final connection. Still, we never gave up hope.

I was unaware then of the behind-the-scenes pressure on Bob from people like Chris Blackwell, who was sending a stream of agents under various guises to "inveigle" Bob into signing a new contract, the first one being no longer valid because of the 1974 breakup of the original Wailers. Bob, using his uncanny, natural ability to avoid pitfalls, was secretly searching for someone to handle these problems, someone with whom he felt a certain "vibe" or affinity. I only discovered later how anxious Bob was about the original Island contract, which he had entered into right after the expiration of his deal with Danny Sims/Cayman Music.

Our busy careers continued to keep Bob and me apart. By 1974, in addition to managing Little Anthony and the Imperials, I had also started to handle Martha Reeves of the Vandellas, who came to me having just signed with Island Records, Bob's recording company.

Island had given Martha an advance against a recording contract. But while the contract was being prepared, Clive Davis, president of Arista Records who had recently signed Barry Manilow, made her a better offer. Martha told me that she wanted to ink the deal with Arista, especially since Island had not created any waves. I set up a meeting with Island Records, intending to try and opt out of the deal by returning the advance.

We met with Charlie Nuccio, then president of Island Records, at the company's Hollywood office. During the meeting Charlie, who was not aware of my Jamaican background, mentioned that he had an artiste on his label who, with work, could be a mega-mega star. But the singer refused to cooperate. When I asked the name of the reluctant artiste, he said "Bob Marley."

More and more lately, I had been hearing Marley's name. In music circles, he and reggae music were frequently being referred to as "the next big thing." In fact, reggae interpretations by talents like Paul Simon, Stevie Wonder, Paul McCartney, the Rolling Stones, Boney M and Abba—to name a few—were becoming commonplace. Reggae was seen as a new music of the oppressed that dealt with politically arousing social issues.

Charlie went on to say that Island Records had recently released Bob's third album, and needed him to go on the road and support it. "Damn!" I said to Charlie, explaining my background and relationship with Bob. "This is the guy who wants to work with me."

Charlie said that he would do anything for anyone who could get Bob to actually work.

My interest renewed, I bundled Martha into my car, dropped her home, and headed straight to my office at 6290 Sunset Boulevard.

My office housed my company—Judant Music Corporation—which I owned jointly with Little Anthony (Anthony Gourdine) and Avco. As company president I was paid $743.52 per week, or $40,000 per year plus expenses, a car, house and entertainment. For a hustler from humble Jamaican beginnings, it was a good start, especially since I could also earn additional income in management.

I caught the next plane to Kingston, plotting my plan of action during the flight. I decided I would go directly by taxi from the Norman Manley Airport at Palisadoes to Bob's home at 56 Hope Road, the address Charlie Nucccio had given me.

I landed in Kingston was between 2:30 and 3:00 p.m. and an hour later had arrived at 56 Hope Road.

I was struck by the impressive old colonial-style house at that address. It was not far from my own apartment and no more than a block from the governor general's residence, King's House, in which visiting kings, queens and presidents had slept. Further down the road was the prime minister's office, the Police Officers' Club, and the Priory School, one of Jamaica's most exclusive. A stone's throw away was Devon House, the home of the first black Jamaican millionaire, Thomas Stiebel.

That Bob Marley, Rastafarian, reggae musician and marijuana smoker, lived in this neighborhood said something about Jamaica under the Manley government, about the gradual acceptance by Jamaicans of black consciousness, their African ancestry, and Rastafarianism.

Later, I discovered that the house had been loaned to Bob by Chris Blackwell, a move I felt was a subtle means of exerting control over his stubborn artiste. Chris and his representatives were also terrified of Trench Town and of the shady characters Bob hung around with in the ghettos of East and West Kingston. The Hope Road location planted Bob in an area more accessible to the overseas press and local media.

On arriving at the house, I saw three or four Rastafarians sitting down and reasoning. I later discovered that Bob was typically surrounded by brethren, members of the Rastafarian religion. The men looked me over with mild suspicion when I asked for Bob, and told me that he was upstairs, asleep. I later learned that it was considered unwise to disturb Bob's sleep. Ignoring their suspicious looks, I headed upstairs and found his room.

A pair of soccer shoes lay on the floor next to the bed, as if awaiting a referee's whistle to leap into action. Behind the bed leaning against the wall was a guitar. Above it, was an imposing portrait of Haile Selassie. Bob was lying on his bed when I stepped into the room and seemed to acknowledge my presence with a slight movement. I touched him and said, "Bob, Don Taylor. I come to manage you now." Rather lazily he sat up, looking at me almost nonchalantly. "Yea Don Taylor," he said, "what deal you want?" I replied, "Twenty per cent." "Wait 'til Allan come dis evening," he replied, "an' you can come back an' we will discuss it." I did not know who Allan was, but I told him I would be back.

Leaving him, I went to my Jamaican home, at the time an apartment on Worthington Avenue, some three miles from Bob's Hope Road premises, where I relaxed and waited for evening.

When I returned to Hope Road, Bob had just finished playing soccer. After showering, he came downstairs, touched me and said, "Don Taylor, mek we discuss dis deal." And so he and I and Allan Cole, whom I was meeting for the first time, negotiated in the yard under a tree.

Allan Cole and Bob seemed to be kindred souls and were physically similar. Like Bob, Cole was tall, lanky, dreadlocked and athletic looking, but shorter. It was plain that a closeness existed between them.

Bob said, "You can get ten per cent, not twenty per cent, and as it grow, it cyaan be on everything." I replied that it had to be on everything. Bob stared at me, then turned and glanced at Cole. Allan listened and seemed to impart his approval without speaking, and after a short pause Bob said, "Blood claat Don Taylor, mi wi work wid yu."

In subsequent discussions, Bob made it plain to me that he was not interested in signing any long-term agreement, but that the job was mine as long as I did it to his satisfaction. That agreement remained between us until his death, when Rita took over the estate.

We arranged to meet eleven o'clock the next day at my apartment. I had had my first lesson in how Bob Marley did business, and in his unique, uncanny way of arriving at a decision.

After leaving Bob, I headed back to my apartment and called Stu Weintraub of Associated Booking, whose agency, I had been told, had wanted to book the upcoming Marley tour. I told Stu that I had already met with Bob at his home, and that details of the upcoming tour would be finalized the following morning in an eleven o'clock meeting. Next I called Charlie Nuccio, the Island president who had been anxious and frustrated over Bob's lack of cooperation, and brought him up to date on developments.

Everyone I spoke with about my plans for Bob, including Stu and Charlie, reacted with skepticism, all saying, "OK. We've heard that before." They obviously don't know DT, I told myself.

I had just finished my coffee the following morning when there was a knock on my door. I opened it and found Bob standing there with a brown-skinned woman. She had sharp, clean, attractive features, wore her hair in locks, and was incongruously dressed in a long white cotton creation. Bob introduced her as Diane Jobson, his attorney.

Bob, Diane and I sat down and discussed the proposed arrangement. I summed up the deal to be his manager that Bob and I had struck the evening before. We confirmed the agreement with a handshake, promising to formally draw up the details later in a management contract. This formal step was never taken; a simple letter from Bob to a booking agent, a copy of which I would receive only years later, in November 1976, was the only written confirmation of my managerial position I ever got.

The discussions with Diane and Bob almost concluded, I called Stu Weintraub and had Bob tell him on the phone that I was now his manager, that he was prepared to go on tour, and that he would do anything I advised.

I then called Charlie at Island Records, told him about the deal, and that Bob and I would be in New York one week later to finalize and verify all the details of the tour. Everyone I contacted was delighted at this turn of events, although I still got the distinct feeling that nobody really expected anything to happen. Apparently Bob had disappointed his handlers before.

But I was not worried. Although Stu and Charlie still felt that Bob would let them down, I had up to then (and always after) found him very cooperative. For obvious reasons, he was cautious and careful. He would often say to me, "Blood claat Don Taylor, dem waan trick mi," and repeatedly I had to assure him that I would never allow him to be tricked or swindled.

To the surprise of all the doubters, Bob began cooperating immediately in planning a tour that would run from the summer 1975 to the end of that year. Its details had to be worked out carefully, allowing for no mishaps or blunders. Bob's career, although at the moment seemingly stuck, simply had great potential.

In 1973, during a tour with Sly Stone, Bob was rumored to have walked off the show. Later I found out that he had left because of a disagreement over stage time. Charlie Nuccio's doubts rang in my ears.

Still, I was confident: the vibes between Bob and me were right. We would begin the tour in Canada and then move on to the rest of North America before taking a break and continuing in Europe, with performances in the UK, France and Spain.

It would be a good start, this tour, to our working relationship. But the real work and the real world still lay ahead. I knew that Bob Marley could do it—that he would force the world to stand up and recognize him. I had little doubt about how I would direct his career.

From here on in, it would be Marley and me.

5

OUR FIRST TOUR AND MY FIRST MEETING WITH CHRIS BLACKWELL

The tour began in Canada with an opening concert scheduled for Massey Hall in Toronto. The promoter was Michael Cole, who would later become the partner and co-owner of the Toronto Maple Leafs. Our arrival the day before the concert was greeted with good publicity because I had ensured that press releases were well prepared and distributed. As the performance neared, I grew in confidence.

On concert night, I just knew, as I drove up to the old-style English concert hall, that this was it—the vibes seemed perfect. The hall was already almost packed to capacity when I entered alone, as was my custom, well in advance of the group to check out last-minute details. That night, the ritual seemed even more important. This was my first Marley concert, and I wanted to make absolutely sure that everything was perfect. It would also be my first opportunity to see Bob Marley perform live and to assess his talent.

Awaiting the arrival of Bob and the group, I stood in the wings watching the other acts with road manager Tony Garnett and the I-Threes—Rita Marley, Judy Mowatt and Marcia Griffiths. Being pregnant at the time, Marcia was threatening to make that group the I-Twos. When it was time for Bob to take the stage I moved to sit alone in back of the hall where I could absorb his performance.

Bob walked on to the stage in what I would later recognize as his inimitable saunter. It was awesome to watch him immediately mesmerize crowd with his presence. His guitar slung over his shoulder, his Rasta locks flowing in unrestricted freedom, he generated a raw power of personality that overwhelmed his worshipers. Sounding his opening refrain "Hail Jah Rastafari!" and without another word, he immediately launched into his opening song, "Concrete Jungle," which brought the crowd to its feet. I watched the audience intently for its reaction as Bob moved smoothly into his follow-up number, "I Shot the Sheriff."

Halfway through the performance, he paused, the audience seeming to hang momentarily in the air, to introduce the brothers in the band. Its members were at that time Family Man Barrett on bass, "Touter" Harvey on keyboards, Carlton Barrett on drums, Al Anderson on lead guitar, Alvin "Seco" Patterson on percussion and Lee Jaffe, who was on harmonica.

After completing his introduction of the band, Bob took a side bow and with his finger pointing to his temple, said "My name is"—pause—the audience held its breath—"some call me natty, some call me dread, some call me natty dread," and as he bellowed this, still holding the finger to his temple, he leaped some six feet into the air as the voices of the thousands roared in thunderous response, "Bob Marley," and in one continuous movement he began performing "Natty Dread."

A superstar was born—I knew that then without a doubt. I never saw Bob use that introduction again throughout the rest of his magical career that grew to immense proportions from that night in Toronto. But he never changed from his trademark introduction of "Hail Jah Rastafari!" which was an opening prayer to Jah, the Rasta name for God.

From Canada, we worked our way down to New York. I had deliberately organized the tour to build up maximum publicity for our New York arrival. Everything worked as I had planned. Reviews poured in from all the majors; the interviews grew in depth and exposure. We hit New York City to much advance notice and acclaim because my public-relations machinery worked perfectly, and my plans fell smoothly into place.

My strategy for our New York arrival called for Bob to play a concert in the summer series in Central Park, which was promoted by Ron Delsner and sponsored by Michelob beer. The show, the first such summer concert ever held, charged a mere two dollars, an admission fee low enough to guarantee a mass turnout that could only widen Bob's audience appeal. The night in the jammed park the concert unfolded like a revival meeting. Underground piracy of reggae tapes in the US had opened up the music, a fact I was banking on and one that very few in the recorded music world seemed to grasp. The well-timed performance in Central Park was perfect for reggae—and for Bob.

We followed up the concert in the park with another New York concert appearance and then moved on.

With New York conquered and behind us, we continued the tour by playing two shows in Philadelphia before moving on to Cleveland, Chicago, Detroit, Seattle, Portland and San Francisco and finally Los Angeles. The reviews everywhere were ecstatic:

> "Bob Marley and the Wailers . . . Reggae at its
> sinuously, sexily rocking best." (John Rockwell,
> NY Times)

"Marley is fantastic, incredible, his lyrics should be printed on the front page of every newspaper." (Dr. John)

"Best thing I have seen in ten years. I could watch the Wailers all night." (George Harrison)

"Marley's exceptional show generated the kind of emotional celebration(some called that kind of experience 'magic'(that results when a performer not only meets the high expectancy level, but actually gives his audience new reasons to believe." (*LA Times*)

"His fans come for the music, but it's the message they take away." (Tom Bradshaw, *LA Times*)

In California we played at the Roxy club on Sunset Boulevard in the heart of Hollywood. I had specifically targeted clubs as part of my plans for Bob's career, knowing that playing them would enhance his reputation by exposing him to new and different audiences. These club appearances were major successes and, together with the acclaimed concerts, cemented Bob's reputation and established a base for renegotiating the second Bob Marley-Island contract. As the tour progressed, I also began to discover the true professional that was Bob Marley: his disciplined approach to the business of music, his preparedness and sense of responsibility and his quick way of learning.

It was in LA that I was to have my first face-to-face meeting with Chris Blackwell. We had proved that we could break into the difficult US market, which up until then had seemed indifferent to reggae. I was ready to take on the world, but first I had to deal with Chris Blackwell.

Because I was negotiating Bob's recording contract with Island, Bob and I had many serious discussions. I had, on assuming managership, reviewed the original contract and concluded that it was a bad deal. Something drastic clearly had to be done if Bob was to be paid what he was worth.

The contract called for Bob to get advances of £4,000 for the first album, £4,000 for the second, and $12,000 for the third. The first two albums had been *Catch a Fire* and *Burnin'*, the third, *Natty Dread*. Astonishingly, however, Bob had not yet received a penny royalty from either album, either as artiste or producer. He had in fact only got the $12,000 for *Natty Dread* after hiring Ray Tisdale, head of business affairs for Capitol Records, and a widely-known lawyer in the music business.

To my mind, the breakup of the original Wailers—Bob, Peter and Bunny—meant that the existing contract was no longer technically and legally binding on Bob Marley as a single artiste. Bob felt the same way and I meant, if necessary, to make this argument the cornerstone of my renegotiation.

In reviewing the strategy for the upcoming negotiations with Bob and Diane, I discovered that Bob had pulled off a masterly business maneuver that attested to his skill as a negotiator.

After the breakup of the original Wailers, Bob had signed a new contract with Island as Bob Marley and the Wailers, naming Family Man Barrett and Carly as members of the new Wailers. He had received an advance of $12,000, advising Ray Tisdale that Family Man and Carly would sign later. Bob then counseled Family Man and Carly not to sign the contract. They followed his advice, with the result that the new contract was of questionable legality because it was not signed by all parties. Bob told me that this move enabled him to take the money but avoid the commitment.

This tactic would backfire years later, when Junior Marvin persuaded Family Man and the other members of the Wailers to claim ownership of the group. They filed a lawsuit in the Supreme Court of Jamaica, even trying to get me to testify, to take over the Wailers band. Bob, however, who had always been wary of Chris Blackwell, had acted out of what he was convinced was his best interest.

In preparing for the renegotiating meeting, I had become increasingly aware of how Bob really felt about Chris. Bob had feelings of foreboding and wanted to quickly extricate himself from the present contract. No doubt, his ambivalence about the contract was behind the uncooperative impression he had given Nuccio and Island.

The meeting to renegotiate Bob's contract with Island was held in July or August of 1975, at the Island Records office in Los Angeles.

Bob and I attended the meeting, accompanied by attorney David Steinberg, who was also acting for Thom Bell, one of the persons who originally brought David and me together. To prepare for the meeting, I had quietly done some limited research on Chris. I was beginning to sense that Blackwell was trying to manipulate events. I just couldn't put my hand on it at the time, but my suspicions were very strong.

After looking me up and down suspiciously, Chris asked me directly what it was I wanted.

I told him I wanted a one-million-US-dollar advance, for which we would give him Bob's next three albums which, added to the three earlier released ones, would make a total of six. Chris countered with his own proposal for ten albums. When Bob asked, "Why do you want so many albums?" Chris said that an artiste's career is usually finished after ten albums. Bob looked Chris over and replied in his most serious voice, "I will give you your ten albums, but I will show you that my career is just beginning after ten albums." Chris laughed.

In this prediction, Chris turned out to be partly right. Bob did die shortly after making his tenth album for Chris. But in his own way, Bob was also right. His career, after a total of ten albums, has really only just begun.

We ended the meeting with nothing settled. I refused to budge from my demands except to agree that Bob would cut ten albums for Chris. Countering, Chris advised us that he would never agree to my terms, that my proposal would not work. He wanted to strike a deal, but not at these terms. We left the meeting with nothing accomplished.

But I was confident that I would win and that we would prevail. I told Bob not to worry, that we would win the battle. Bob was noncommittal. His usual tactic was never to say yes or no to any proposal, but to leave the final decision to you—if for no other reason than to later hold you responsible. This approach created its own problems. People who asked him to participate in a business deal, would often be vaguely told, "Mi think it wi work," which would be mistaken for a commitment. Later, they would come to me for money and end up blaming me for blocking the deal.

Meanwhile, under my management, Bob continued to grow in stature and recognition. He was playing the right places, making all the right moves. Mick Jagger, who was then also appearing in Los Angeles, cut short his own concert to see Bob perform. Word got out around L.A. that Bob's show was the best.

I saw the future looming ahead bright and clear. Bob had told me that he would like to tie up the deal with Blackwell and get on with cutting albums. He further confided to me that Chris had made a back-door appeal to him in the capacity of a friend. As Bob put it, Chris had said, "Bob, me and you is friend, whey yu bring this bwoy from to mash up our business." Although I respected their previous association, I was determined that no future Island contract with Bob would ever again be onesided, with Chris Blackwell as the major beneficiary.

As a precaution and an alternative, I decided to generate interest in Bob from Clive Davis, head of Arista Records (the same person who had been interested in Martha Reeves). Arista was then being financed by Polygram Records from Germany and hungry for new talent. Over the years, Clive had developed the reputation of being one of the best record men in the business; many even regarded him as the messiah of modern-day music.

As a former president of CBS Records, Clive had a nose for the right musical trends. He was interested in signing Bob and promised that if we got into a lawsuit with Island, he would fund the fight. I bided my time and waited. Soon Blackwell must come to realize that he could no longer exploit this situation to his benefit only, but would have to deal.

About two or three days after this first meeting with Chris, we left LA for London to begin the European leg of the tour. Arriving in London early the next morning, we were met by an Island assistant, Denise Mills, who insisted that Bob and I go straight to Island to meet with Chris Blackwell.

I had already figured out that Chris, knowing nothing about me, had used the few days to do a background check. No doubt he would try to find out, for instance, if I could be swayed in my judgment by lavish wining and dining. The apparent haste with which he had called the second meeting made it clear to my mind that he now knew that I was ground-ed in the music business, had contact with the right people, and that it was in his best interest to begin negotiating in good faith. I was not going to be a pushover; the days of one-sided deals with Bob Marley and Island were over.

Bob and I had discussed alternative bargaining ploys, and he had taken his usual noncommittal position. I entered the new discussions knowing that Bob wanted to be free of his contractual commitments to Island, but feeling also that, for old times' sake, he was willing to give Chris the albums, if only to be rid of him once and for all.

Bob was Island—that was also becoming clear to me. And I was finding it difficult to forget that we were dealing with the same Chris Blackwell who had earlier financed the pirating of Jamaican reggae music and Marley recordings through a deal with Trojan Records and Lee Gopthals. This information had come out earlier from Bob's and Lee "Scratch" Perry's trips to London.

We arrived at Island's office in St. Peter's Square, near Hammersmith, a converted old English house not unlike Bob's home at 56 Hope Road, in Kingston. Opposite Island's offices, I can clearly recall, was a big bingo parlor catering to the craze at the time in England. Denise escorted us to Chris's little office in the back which was cluttered with recording industry paraphernalia.

Chris was waiting for us, dressed in his usual unassuming style—tennis shoes and no socks. Without too many opening pleasantries, Chris said, "OK, let's try and put something together." I felt a great sense of gratification at being right. It was as I thought: Chris had found out about Don Taylor and Don Taylor's savvy of the music industry.

I laid out to Chris what I wanted, which was merely a repetition of my earlier demands, but with a new request to purchase the premises at 56 Hope Road.

I had been thinking about Hope Road for quite some time and felt that the time was ripe for Bob to purchase it. Chris said that a purchase was not necessary, because the house was Bob's to use as he wanted. This arrangement made me uneasy, smacking as it did of the slave master housing his slave. "You can stay there as long as you are a good boy" was what that proposal sounded like to me. I told Chris emphatically I did not want Bob living under that kind of understanding, and that we had to buy the house. Chris must have seen my resolve, which was seconded by Bob, because he agreed to agree to sell us the premises for US$125,000.

Matters between us, however, were not so simply resolved, and this back-and-forth pattern would prove to be typical of Chris's style of negotiating with us. Two days later, when we went to sign the contract, Chris produced a statement claiming that Bob owed Island $550,000. He said that the money had been advanced over the years to the Wailers. This alarming figure contrasted sharply with the money that Bob, Peter Tosh and Bunny Wailer could actually remember receiving—a mere £8,000 and $12,000.

I asked Chris to pull the account records on the figures and was not really surprised to find that the money supposedly received on behalf of Bob Marley and the Wailers had, in every instance, been signed for by people employed by Chris Blackwell.

I found this method of payment highly unusual. Normally, when a record company pays out large sums of money, it requires the same signatures that appear on the contract, not those of representatives or its own employees.

In reality, Chris had waited too long to begin to deal with me on the contract. Thanks to my shrewd management and teamwork, Bob stature was growing. The tour had been a huge success. Bob's natural lifestyle, his unchoreographed moves and raw talent were mesmerizing the world; his lyrics and message were winning hearts and souls. To use Bob's parlance, the world was beginning to "overstand" his message.

It was also apparent to me, especially from these meetings, that Chris now realized that Bob's best works were still ahead of him. I can recall Bob telling him, "If yu give me a good deal you get good records, if you give me a bad deal I give you a bad record." Chris had smiled. He must have known that he had given Bob a bad deal before and had still gotten three great records.

After reviewing the amount allegedly owed to Island, I refused outright to pay it even if the debt were divided equally between Bob, Bunny and Peter Tosh. I don't know if Chris even pressed a similar claim on Bunny and Peter Tosh, both of whom had already left the Wailers for independent careers, although I think it unlikely either would have agreed to pay it. For my part, I stood firm on the issue and Chris finally agree to waive Bob's alleged share of $175,000, a lot of money then and now in any currency (at the time the Jamaican dollar was worth eighty cents US).

On finalizing the million-dollar contract that called for a twenty-five per cent advance of $250,000, I advised Chris to deduct $125,000 for Hope Road and draw a check for the difference of $125,000. Everyone, including Bob, was pleased at the amicable outcome.

We proceeded to complete the UK leg of the tour, staging three shows at the Lyceum in London, resulting in Bob's first live recorded album: *Live!* These concerts helped launch the song "No Woman No Cry," previously recorded on the *Natty Dread* album, Bob's debut as a solo artiste. Both the *Live!* album and "No Woman No Cry" made the charts.

By this time the press releases and interviews had had their desired impact, and the rest of Europe began to clamor for Bob. We had to bring in reporters from all over Europe for a press conference that was held at the Kensington Hotel during which we promised to tour other European countries the following year.

Before returning home in triumph, we completed the tour by going from London to Birmingham and Manchester. Bob and I grew closer, and he expressed his satisfaction at my management style and confidence in my ability to take his career to a new height.

6

MANAGING BOB

Bob mistrusted everybody—during the first years of my management that became clear. His mistrust was, I guessed, based on bad experiences with the people closest to him and with others in the music industry and the recording business in Jamaica. He simply mistrusted everybody. Because I was the one who was making the deals and making all the money for him, over time I gradually gained a little more of his trust. But Bob still had his own way of checking up on people.

At the close of our first year together, with Bob's star continuing to rise, I decided that the time had come to reexamine our whole accounting structure. The contract with Island was London based and thus subject to UK taxes. As record sales climbed and increased our income, Bob suddenly found himself in the 70 to 80 percent bracket of British taxpayers, the highest.

I decided to discuss the matter with Marvin Zolt whose accounting services I had used when I managed Little Anthony and the Imperials. Into my management team, I brought the later infamous team of David Steinberg, as lawyer, and Marvin Zolt, as accountant. My exposure to the intricacies of the music business over the years had taught me long ago that you needed whites to deal with whites. I held a meeting with Zolt and Steinberg about Bob's tax situation and was referred to a contact person in DC, a client of theirs, who in turned referred me in 1975 to a tax lawyer, one Jerome Kurtz.

After getting Bob's approval, I hired Kurtz at $7,000 per day to come to New York and advise us what to do about taxes.

Kurtz traveled from Washington to New York, examined our situation, and advised us to establish a company on the island of Tortola in the British Virgin Islands. This country, he said, through a treaty with the USA that dated back to 1939, was exempted by law from the US tax code. The law allowed any company registered in Tortola, and owned and managed out of Tortola, to exempt all its earnings in commission or royalties from taxes both in the US and UK. He further advised that Bob's earnings could be moved from the US and the UK to Tortola without tax penalty and gave me the name of a attorney in Tortola, one Michael Regiles, who could set up the company.

We urgently needed to make this move in light of the renegotiated Island contract. During this time, I also had a feeling that Chris's company was not prospering. None of his other recording artistes was selling any records. His other potential star, Steve Winwood of Traffic, wasn't doing particularly well because he wouldn't work. In fact, Bob was his best-selling artiste.

With this leverage, I tried dictating to Island the terms I wanted and began taking unusual risks. For example, during our London tour, we had recorded *Live!*, but because a live recording was not covered by the Island contract, Chris refused to accept it as part of our deal. We therefore needed a company that would own it outright. I had demanded a lot of money from Island for distribution rights to this album, but

Chris had refused to pay, creating an impasse between us. Despite this impasse, Chris had Island release the album in the UK only, which led to another confrontation.

I immediately demanded payment for the UK rights, as well as a further payment for the European rights. We got a substantial sum—as I recall about $500,000—a payment that did not make Chris very happy.

This situation and other developments clearly called for another meeting between Chris, Bob, Steinberg and me. I called Michael Regiles, the recommended lawyer in Tortola, who advised me that he had an already formed company, Media Aides, that he could sell us for $1,000. I immediately sent a check to pay for the cost of the company and to open a company account at Barclays Bank in Tortola.

Forming this new company now gave me the opportunity I needed to try to correct the situation with not only Chris Blackwell and Island, but also with Danny Sims about Bob's publishing rights that Danny had placed in Cayman Music.

What had happened was this: when Bob had been signed by Cayman Music, which was owned by Danny and "Big" Paul Castellano, the contract gave Danny control of management, recordings and publishing of Bob's music. The songs involved included "Guava Jelly," later recorded by Barbra Streisand, and "I Shot the Sheriff," an early Eric Clapton hit, and other Marley classics such as "Get Up Stand Up" and "Reggae on Broadway."

The earnings from these records were to be accounted for by Copyright Service Bureau, run by a lawyer, Walter Hoffer. His actions created and compounded the problem and would later cause a confrontation between Danny, the Mafia and me.

When Bob saw that the publishing rights from "I Shot the Sheriff" amounted to about nine million dollars, he became

suddenly aware of the value of the rights he had assigned to
Cayman Music and began to suspect that Danny was keeping
earnings from him. To escape Cayman's publishing ownership,
he decided, with Allan Cole and Yvette Morris (then an
employee and one-time girlfriend of Bob), to put the names of
other people on his songs. All the songs on the *Natty Dread*
album used other names, including the single "No Woman No
Cry."

In his characteristic way, by hanging around with Danny,
Bob had begun to get the hang of the intricacies of the music
business. He began to learn about the difference between
managing, publishing and recording. When the contract with
Danny came up for renewal, Bob agreed to extend the publishing rights for another year if Danny would release the
recording and management parts of the contract back to him.

Once again Bob had absorbed the goings-on until he
learned enough to make his own demands.

Danny agreed to this change, and Bob proceeded, with the
help of Allan Cole and Yvette Morris, to form a series of companies under the name Tuff Gong (the name of the original
company he had formed and owned jointly with Bunny Wailer
and Peter Tosh). Tuff Gong Music, USA, was thus created and
registered in the USA as a distinctly separate entity to Tuff
Gong Distributions Jamaica, Tuff Gong Music, also registered
in Jamaica, or Tuff Gong Records and Tuff Gong Productions,
which I formed and registered in Tortola. To this US company
Bob, Allan and Yvette assigned the earnings of the new songs.

Inheriting this scenario, I realized at once that they had
made two glaring errors: first they should not have registered
the company in the USA because doing so made its earnings
taxable; and second the company's registration showed Yvette
owning a 99-percent share with only 1 percent going to Bob.

After advising Bob of these errors, I proceeded to correct them.

Because I knew that in the music business the real power lies with the person who collects the money, I proceeded to register a new company, Bob Marley Music, in Tortola, and assign all earnings to this company, making them nontaxable. I also corrected the registration of the company so that Yvette Morris no longer owned 99 per cent.

We had just completed the *Rastaman Vibration* album, and it had come out at the same time that the contract with Danny Sims had expired. To escape Danny Sims's ownership, Bob and I decided to put some of the new songs under the names of fictitious writers.

But because we needed to retain Bob's visibility as a songwriter, I carefully selected the songs that I would ascribe to others. I placed such names as Allan Cole, Carlton Barrett, Family Man Barrett and Rita Marley on the songs recorded for the Rastaman Vibration album, the jacket of which read:

Bob Marley & The Wailers
Rastaman Vibration
Bob Marley Music
(Media Aides Ltd. Tortola)

The writers were listed thus:

SONGS	WRITERS
Positive Vibration	V. Ford
Roots, Rock, Reggae	V. Ford
Johnny Was	R. Marley
Cry to Me	R. Marley
Want More	A. Barrett

Crazy Baldhead	R. Marley, V. Ford
Who the Cap Fit	A. Barrett, C. Barrett
Night Shift	Bob Marley
War	A. Cole, C. Barrett
Rat Race	R. Marley

Changing the songwriters' names did not affect the collection of revenue, as Bob's company or Bob was the publisher in every case, and all the songwriters were listed at the same address. When checks payable to the fictitious writers arrived, we simply endorsed them and deposited them in the Tortola account. Frequently, the writer would be listed on the album as "R. Marley, writer," which could be either Robert Marley or Rita Marley, in whose names many of the songs were also registered. This tactic allowed me to keep current Bob's visibility as a songwriter while disguising his income and earnings as a songwriter from any other company that might otherwise claim them.

This kind of strategic management of a performer's business affairs is an important part of being a manager, and I felt proud of the way I was protecting Bob's earnings and overseeing his career growth. Until I took over as Bob's manager, Island Records had been mainly profiting.

By now we had some five bank accounts reflecting substantial earnings. In fact, the Tortola account at that time had deposits of up to ten million US dollars.

My spectacular success predictably made me enemies, and I found myself constantly beset from all sides. As Bob grew in stature and fame, many people who felt they could do my job better pressured him to get rid of me, concocting lies that I was robbing him.

I had to deal with constant newcomers appearing almost out of nowhere, while trying at the same time to cope with the old hands at the game such as Danny Sims.

Danny never gave up trying to get back in the driver's seat or to prove that he was being cheated. He was always trying to influence Bob through people who would front for him. I remember one time during a tour that a Zimbabwean, Joe Stebleski, appeared out of the blue claiming that he was an accountant with Danny Sims. He insisted on meeting with our accountant in New York, Marvin Zolt, with the aim of proving to Bob that I was stealing from him. This charge was, of course, a two-edged sword, for trying to prove veiled accusations against me could expose the songwriters' scam, which we maintained with Bob's knowledge and approval. Sims and company seemed to suspect that new songs were being registered in the names of fictitious songwriters.

There was also continuous pressure from Chris Blackwell, whose tactic was to keep two or three people continuously purveying rumor and carrying news. Although many people have claimed that genuine friendship existed between Bob and Chris, I never saw it in all the discussions, conversations and exchanges that I had with Bob. Without any fear of contradiction, I can categorically state that no such friendship existed. What Chris and Bob had between them was mutual respect for each other's professional and creative abilities. But there was no friendship. In fact, I don't think Bob liked Chris.

Using the classic method of money making, Chris tried to exert complete control over his artistes by not only recording them, but also being their manager and publisher. He wanted this kind of control over Bob but couldn't get it because Bob was the smarter of the two.

Although Chris also grew up in Jamaica, the two men came from very different cultures. Chris represented everything that Bob was against. Under the tutelage of his mother Blanche Blackwell, an heir to the Crosse & Blackwell fortune, Chris had formed Island Records (named, some would say, after Alec Waugh's novel *Island in the Sun*) in 1959 and opened its London office in 1962.

Chris had seen Bob's first two albums, *Catch a Fire* (1973) and *Burnin'*, which boasted such tracks as "Get Up Stand Up" and "I Shot the Sheriff," meet with a strong response from the music world. And Chris had an ear for any music that was not mainstream. In fact, he shied away from traditional, mainstream material.

Because no one knew the real value of new, innovative music, this emphasis gave Chris an advantage, allowing him to exploit ignorant artistes, paying them only what he wished. With no other guiding light or historic precedent, Chris himself determined value. And since most nontraditional and non-mainstream music was coming from the so-called Third World, where music publishing and copyright were not well understood by the lawyers much less by the musicians themselves, he was able to get the best out of these musicians before they became popular.

In fact, he would get the best out of them at a very low cost and before they understood what he was doing. Such is the typical approach and practice of independent music companies. It is their classic way of operating in the music world.

It wasn't surprising, then, that the musical talents in Chris's stable achieved financial success usually only after they had left him; the careers of performers like Steve Winwood, Robert Palmer, Joe Cocker, Jimmy Cliff, and Cat Stevens, to name a few artistes who formed part of his Island anglo-rock era from 1969 to 1972, exemplify this truth.

Another reason Marley and Chris could never be truly close was the vast gulf in their personal lives. Chris, although not gay himself, had many gay and bisexual friends whom Bob, like most Jamaican macho men, abhorred. Nor did it help their relationship when Bob realized that Chris had given him an unfair deal on his first two albums.

Take *Catch a Fire*, which still sells today. By any standards, this album was a spectacular success. By my own reckoning, its sales must have been well over two million copies. Yet for that and two other albums, as far as I know, Chris paid the Wailers £8,000 and $12,000.

As Bob said in June 1975, "Wasn't because of no connection that we go to England [for a recording contract]. The guys we used to deal with in England was some big pirates. Them guys kill off reggae music, kill rock steady and kill ska. Them guys for reggae music like some people is for rock, y'know, suck out the artist and sometimes them kill them."

Bob told me he resented that Chris was always trying to put his own name on to Bob's work as producer, a title that was inaccurate. Chris may occasionally have contributed an idea— he did this from time to time—but he never produced.

Just for the record—no pun intended—on the first contract between Bob and Island, Chris paid Bob eight percent and himself two percent as producer, although he was not really the producer. But then, such are the traps awaiting the unsuspecting and the ignorant in the music world.

Take the case of Trojan Records. Without authorization, this company put out all the early Bob Marley records in England. Try as we did, neither Bob nor I could get them to

render royalty statements or make royalty payments. We tried
to find the source of their organization and distribution but
without luck. Eventually, we discovered that Chris was a
shareholder in Trojan, that he had formed the company with
Lee Gopthals, an Indian from Delhi, and was, in reality, par-
ticipating in the piracy.

My research revealed that in 1968 or thereabouts Chris
merged his business with a company called B&C Records that
used to handle all the releases generated by the leading
Jamaican labels and producers, including the Upsetters, Duke
Reid, Harry J, Treasure Isle, Leslie Kong and Coxsone Dodd.
I estimate that this company handled some fifty labels in all—
little short of piracy.

Because of the way Chris's business was structured, no one
could figure out who was doing what. Deals were signed on
top of deals; no one knew who was selling, producing, licens-
ing or distributing what. His organization was a true hydra-
headed monster. Discovering the extent of Chris's deceit made
me extremely cautious in dealing with him and more determined than ever to regain ownership of all that was rightfully
Bob's.

In 1976 Bob said, "Yes, people rob me and try fe trick me,
but now I have experience. Now I know and I see and I don't
get tricked. Used to make recordings and not get royalties.
Still happen sometime. All Wailers records made here
[Jamaica] but then pirated to England. All them English companies rob man. Everybody that deals with West Indian
music—thieves."

For myself, I have no deep resentment of Chris; he played
his part. And as distributor, he eventually opened up his check-
book and allowed me to run the show. Not the creative genius
that everybody tries to make him out to be, Chris, however,

earned more than his fair share. His true genius is as a smart businessman, a fact that Bob recognized. He was always anxious to finish the contracted albums and would often say to me, "Don Taylor when we a go finish these albums and get rid of this man."

Chris and the atmosphere he created were not to Bob's liking. More and more this fact became evident. Indeed, as time passed, it became clear to Chris that Bob was becoming independent of him, especially financially. In the 1975/76 period, for example, when we were due some $2.2 million in royalties, we discovered that Chris and Island were tight on cash. Bob and I agreed, at Chris's request, to not demand the royalties that were due. To help Chris weather the storm and keep the company going, Bob left the money in Island in the form of a loan.

As time passed, then, Chris had been reduced to being a mere distributor, a reality that I always felt he resented. Chris had to have things his own way and would rather see you off the scene if he couldn't.

Bob really wanted to be rid of Chris. He wanted to own himself totally, to harness his creativity for his own children rather than for Chris Blackwell. It was an ambition he never stopped emphasizing to me.

Once I realized how important this goal was to Bob, I made up my mind to work hard and speed up the delivery of the contracted albums to Island.

In the meantime, I had to deal with the unhurried Jamaican scene and make my way through Bob's way of life. It was a way of life which, in contrast to the hectic touring days, was slow-moving and unpretentious.

Indeed, it was very much unlike the pace I had learned to live with in LA.

7

THE JAMAICAN SCENE

On his return to Jamaica in late 1975, Bob was resoundingly welcomed in spite of the ideological and political passions raging throughout the island. His musical achievements and his remarkable lyrics had struck a responsive chord with Jamaicans. He was on his way to becoming a living legend.

He settled into a routine as normal as possible for Bob Marley. He began to feel more personally connected to his residence at 56 Hope Road now that he owned it outright. It was not easy for the world to understand Bob's laid-back attitude, his unpretentious and open Jamaican lifestyle. Megastars from the UK and USA were frequently baffled by the way he lived.

On a normal day, Bob would wake early, usually before anyone else, no matter what the night before had entailed, and almost always begin rehearsing immediately—alone. He would stop for breakfast, prepared by his personal hired cook, Gillie. Bob had few preferences for his food, so long as it was ital (cooked without salt), and did not include pork or any other meat, as he was virtually a vegetarian. He ate meat only rarely, a regimen that served him well when he was placed on a rigid diet after the discovery of his cancer.

Religiously starting his day with a mug of porridge, usually cornmeal, he would sip it while reading the Bible, another daily practice. His Bible was always kept nearby during his rehearsals.

As the day wore on, the entourage of visitors would descend, ranging from members of the band to musical associates such as Tommy Cowan or business people like Colin Leslie and Diane Jobson.

Diane was a fairly typical example of an upper-class woman completely under his control. She was a real uptown girl, whom Bob had taken and bred into the Rasta faith in the early seventies and, after he got bored with her, gave the day-to-day task of being his lawyer. She must have resented my arrival on the scene and my relationship with Bob, over whose accounts and transactions I had assumed total control.

I now knew so much about his business that the bank would often call for my okay of his checks. My entry into his affairs caused enmity and bitter blood among those who had preceded me in Bob's life. No doubt, this resentment sparked the swirling rumors and stories, which still linger in the minds of many, that I was cheating Bob. The stories were nonsense, of course, and exactly the kind of envious tales any successful manager can expect.

Arriving around ten in the morning, a stream of hangers-on would descend on the house, usually with open and outstretched hands that never seemed satisfied. The throng would set off an endless round of cooking, eating, and smoking of weed lasting until three or four in the afternoon when all would leave to play soccer on the front lawn of Hope Road or at a nearby playing field.

From far and wide the people came. Some were adherents of the Rasta religion, some ghetto strongmen, some political enforcers or plain hustlers. Bob had become such a soft touch that he was like Santa Claus reincarnated for the hordes of seekers. Bob ignored every attempt I made to put a stop to this begging until suddenly one day he realized that he had given away one million dollars in two months. He quickly came to his senses and began walking around with his trousers' pockets turned out, a signal that the giveaway was ended.

Shortly after this change of heart, he told me that he wanted to expand the Tuff Gong Group of Companies to include a recording and record manufacturing company. To this end, I registered Tuff Gong Distributors (Jamaica), and Tuff Gong Recording (Jamaica), pleased that Bob seemed to have decided that instead of giving money away, he would provide work for those who wanted it.

In an era when there were no videos, satellite dishes or CDs, Bob was, without a doubt, unique in his approach to life, to music, and in his behavior after he became a star.

One of his most precious moments, he always told me, occurred in 1975 as we were flying by private plane into Philadelphia for our concert, arriving at the same time as the Pope. On hearing that the Pope's plane was held up by the tower to allow us to land, Bob turned to me and, with seriousness, said, "Don Taylor, you see who is God pickney, see how them hold up the man for I."

> Babylon system is the vampire
> Sucking the blood of the sufferers. . .
> ("Babylon System")

Although Bob lived close to the edge, smoking weed was the only illegal act I had ever known him to do. But smoking the weed being part of his religion, he did it openly before the highest representatives of law and order, even before prime ministers and church leaders, without any charges ever being brought against him in Jamaica. He was probably one of the few entertainers who had the provision and supply of marijuana written into his contracts. Indeed his "normal" use of marijuana, especially in the context of his clean, clear, and honest political beliefs, probably explained why his ganja smoking was so widely accepted. Eventually even I, unknown to him, tried to keep him supplied with weed. I remember an occasion when, on the Japan tour, I smuggled weed through customs in my boots. Not for nothing was Bob "Tuff Gong," which was ghetto speak for "Tough Shit."

During this period in Jamaica, I also got to know both the original Wailers as well as the shifting assortment of musicians who later played in that band.

I soon came to understand why the original Wailers, whose members were uniquely different personalities, had broken up. Peter Tosh was very negative about Chris Blackwell, especially after the Wailers' disappointing earnings from the albums *Burnin'* and *Catch a Fire*. Bunny was an individualist. Once the adoration of the fans became centered not on the group as a whole but mainly on Bob, it was inevitable that a band consisting of such strong personalities should split apart. With Peter's deep radicalism and dislike of Blackwell coupled with Bunny's strong individualism, the breakup of the Wailers was foreordained.

The Wailers may have left Bob, but Bob never felt that he had ever left the Wailers. He made it clear that he regarded Tuff Gong as still including its original three members: himself, Bunny and Peter. I recall the time when Diane Jobson wanted to take the names of Peter and Bunny off the company only to be told by Bob, "We are still Tuff Gong, it started with me, Peter and Bunny, and we no split."

Bob fully shared Peter Tosh's feeling about Chris Blackwell. But unlike Peter, Bob was always conscious of the need for timing—to pick the right moment to deal with any problem. It became clear to me that Bob intended to grapple with Blackwell only after he felt that the two of them stood on even ground. That moment came after the *Natty Dread* album. It was then that we renegotiated the original contract.

Bob's relationship with members of the later Wailers lacked the depth of feeling he felt for the original cast. Indeed, it varied with his ability to relate to the individual musician's talent and ideas. He said:

> "If you play music, or listen to music and you don't know why you're playing or listening except for money and pleasure, you can be in serious trouble. Reggae say something if it mean something to the people who make it and the people who listen to it." (June 1975)

The members of the later Wailers was a mixed crew.

There was Willie Lindo, who flitted in and out of the group, and one time even left to tour with Taj Mahal, which really pissed off Bob.

There was Tyrone Downie, whom Bob liked, and who brought him music gathered from all over the globe. Bob felt a great affinity with him and considered Tyrone "a young and progressive musician." He compared Tyrone favorably to Family Man and Carlton, both of whom he felt were trapped in the "one drop" concept of reggae music.

I continually marveled at Bob's uncanny ability to predict the trends and modes he needed to code into his music. I noted how careful he was about not trying to change anyone who was unwilling to change. Yet he was always sensitive to those band members who wished to expand their own musical horizons. For example, when Bob became interested in punk rock and wanted to "mesh" it with reggae to record "Punky Reggae Party," he met stiff resistance from many in the band, especially from Family Man. Instead of fighting to change their minds, Bob simply went to London with Lee Perry and recorded "Punky Reggae Party" with Rico Rodriguez's band. To everyone's amazement, it became a smashing success, elevating Bob into the mass musical movement. Because Tyrone had strongly backed the experiment, Bob felt especially close to him afterwards. As Bob said about his musical taste:

> "Soul, jazz, reggae, calypso, blues—I like plenty good music. Jazz, that's a complete music. Music with feeling . . . don't like music or anything that deals with the wrong things of life, because I only want to deal with the truth." (June 1976)

Few band members felt so impartial about their music. In fact, Family Man used to say that he would play no music but "rockers." Carlton, for his part, said very little but invariably tried to do whatever Bob wanted. And what Bob wanted was made clear in his view of reggae music:

> "You get to appreciate [recognize] the foolish ones, the guys play reggae skanop, skanop,

skanop. Not my type of reggae that. My reggae unncha cha, unncha cha, unncha cha, more
rootsie." (June 1976)

Al Anderson played for the later Wailers as a hired musi-
cian, toured with us in 1975, was almost always available when
Bob needed him, but kept demanding more and more money
than Bob was willing to pay. Al, who was an American, and
Bob eventually failed to see eye to eye on certain issues. His
monetary demands finally forced us to bring in Donald
Kinsey, who remained with us through 1976, until the time
Bob and I were shot in the attempted assassination. In fact,
Donald was rehearsing at the time of the shooting.

Al's demands for money were completely unjustified
because, to protect his rights to his music, Bob always overpaid
his musicians. Everyone who played for Bob earned top dollar.

The story of how Donald was hired as a replacement for
Al Anderson demonstrates the shrewd and calculating business
side of Bob Marley.

Al Anderson was making wild demands on Bob for royalties; in fact, he wanted the moon. Bob told him that he would
send me to London, where Al was touring, to negotiate with
him. Bob's words to him were, "Listen man, everything yuh
waan yuh will get, but I am going to sen' Donald Taylor there,
an' yuh can work it out, an' when Donald Taylor gets there,
Donald Taylor will hook up a call, an' I will work it out an'
clear it up."

To me Bob said, "Listen, when yuh get to England an'
meet with Al, whatever yuh seh, yuh going to seh to me over
the phone, an' I am going to say yes; but listen for a knocking
sound on the phone." He picked up the phone and knocked on

the mouthpiece. "When I knock twice, that means 'no.' Even when I say 'yes.' In the end you will advise Al dat yuh will get back to him."

We never did get back to Al. And the ruse left him with the distinct impression that it was I, not Bob, who had refused to meet his demands.

The last addition to the later Wailers was Junior Marvin, who came on board after the free concert in 1976. He was only a hired musician yet has since had the gall to make claims against Bob's music and royalty earnings. I recall Bob once telling Junior, "A bring yuh to Jamaica, tek de earring out a yuh ear, gi yuh a house an a woman. What more yuh waan?" Bob saw Junior as a musician who, though not his equal in talent, was nevertheless always trying to upstage him.

In actuality, none of the musicians in the band ever knew exactly how much they would be paid. Bob would just say, "Dis man get dat, and dat man get dat." But everyone was, in every instance, overpaid.

And the musicians knew it. In all my time with Bob Marley, I never heard Carly or Family Man ask for more money. But Al and Junior Marvin, who were considered outsiders, did.

Sometimes Bob would tell them that he was trying to protect them against themselves because they spent their money so fast. Al, and later on Junior, took this attitude to mean that more money was available but being deliberately withheld, causing a conflict. Neither one, however, had the guts to openly say anything on the subject matter to Bob. Instead, they all took out their bitterness on me.

Bob was a sensitive and funny man who always gave people the opportunity to speak and listened to what they had to say before trying to assess them. His closest friend was undoubtedly Allan "Skill" Cole, who has always been known for being thrifty. One day, shortly after he had won a large sum of money at the races, Skill asked Bob to lend him $10,000. I can still see Bob's friendly reaction and hear the affection in his voice when he said, "Rass claat, Skill, yuh mean yuh just win so much money and rather than use that yuh want borrow from me!"

It took me the first year—specifically the combination of the first tour along with the time spent in Jamaica—to really grasp how Bob functioned. I learned that he was the only man who could speak for the Wailers, that he never said a direct yes or no to any idea. Instead, he would say vaguely, "It sounds like it could work," never anything more definite and committed such as, "It will definitely work." If your plan then misfired, you were guilty and Bob blameless. I also found that Bob liked to have money but only for the freedom it gave him to be himself and to be free of debt, a cardinal wish of his life.

Our relationship grew closer and prospered over the years in spite of the fact that Bob trusted nobody and thought everybody dishonest.

Bob had one burning desire: to lead a revolutionary assault on the forces of Babylon by giving voice to the downtrodden and the oppressed through his music. He seemed to understand that the army arrayed in the struggle against Babylon must comprise united elements of the political culture and the Rastafarian religion.

It soon became clear to me that Bob Marley had become the leader and focus of a disenfranchised army of dissidents, toughs, gunmen and political enforcers of both political parties—JLP and PNP. Leading the whole army was a general—Allan "Skill" Cole—with Bob as the chief of staff who financed the operations, kept dissidents in line, and plotted Babylon's defeat.

Bob was obsessed with the challenge of welding into one unified organization the increasingly divided Rastafarian tribes and the warring political activists whose constant violent confrontations were growing in intensity and viciousness. Bob wanted to demonstrate to the people of Jamaica, and indeed the world, that opposing parties could live together in peace and mutual respect. "God never made no difference between black, white, blue, pink or green. People is people, yuh know. That is the message we try to spread."

Once I asked him whether the politicians knew about him and his ambitions. He replied, "Yeah man. They nuh like me 'cause I talk against de system. Some of dem seh, 'Well Bob you're nice.' They are looking for me like aluminum, Jamaica's main export, y'know, so I can bring back some money in. I'm not interested in that, I'm interested in what's happening to the people. I mean I really like to walk down the street, and everyone smile at me, instead of suffer. Guys suffer so much, they don't have time to smile. The politicians cause it."

His dream of uniting opposing Jamaican factions motivated him to take ardent political opponents into his day-to-day life and, later, on the tours. In a practical way, he wished to show them that it was possible, in his presence, to live, eat and sleep with the enemy without antagonisms and suspicions. Consequently, we almost always had in residence two important generals of the street and political ghettos, Claudie Massop and Tony Welch. To Bob, their presence represented the hope of unification in this most bitterly divided time.

Claudie Massop was a noted front-line organizer for Eddie Seaga, leader of the then opposition Jamaica Labor Party. Athletically built and some six feet tall, with sharp appealing looks and a winning smile, Massop was a supremely tough enforcer, but with an endearing underlying soft, gentle side.

Tony Welch, on the other hand, was a leading fixer for the PNP. Five foot seven, slim and brown-skinned, he had been introduced to Bob by Tony Spaulding, for whom he was an equally efficient enforcer. Representing the bitterly opposed sides, these two political operatives presented a constant challenge to Bob's hopes and desires. Through them Bob glimpsed a way to cope with Babylon, the common enemy.

Bob gave them virtually anything they wanted. On one trip to Miami, for example, Bob bought Tony a BMW. Tony was supposed to pay him back, but as far as I recall, never did.

To a sociologist, I suppose Bob would seem a man trying to use his money and power to mobilize the masses into a revolution—whether mental or physical. Maintaining ties with both political factions in Jamaica was also Bob's way of playing it safe in the volatile political atmosphere of 1970s Jamaica.

Bob also attempted social unification of the Rasta religion, whose members always played a significant role in his life, and he took seriously the continued war being waged against them by Babylon. Around this time, some eight Rastas had their locks forcibly shorn in Kingston, increasing tensions and leading to the formation of "Jah Rastafari Holy Theocratic Government." Out of this movement, with Bob's help, came a thirteen-member delegation that called for a series of meetings with Prime Minister Manley to improve relationships between what they called, "yovernments."

These events impressed upon Bob that a greater effort was needed to heal the social wounds and close the gaping economic gap in Jamaica.

After Bob intervened, the Rastas settled in Bull Bay, not far from the small government-built house that was his other residence. This house, which Bob had settled in after moving from Trench Town, is in itself an interesting story.

Bob had gotten the house through Tony Spaulding, the MP for Trench Town, who was so close to him that Bob could later speak of various favors he had received from politicians. (Their closeness also made me understand those underground stories once in circulation about the political strong-arm payola that had gotten Bob's music played on the radio during the early years.) Until his move to Bull Bay with Skill Cole and Marcia Griffiths, Bob had never owned a house. Afterwards, he would spend his time between Trench Town, Bull Bay, and 56 Hope Road.

Bob soon formed a solid relationship with the Rastas he had helped move to Bull Bay. They, in turn, influenced the *Rastaman Vibration* album that proclaimed his adoption of the Twelve Tribes beliefs—that he was of the tribe of Joseph, his color was white, and his blessing would come from Genesis 49:22-24, and Deuteronomy 33:16: "Joseph was a fruitful bough."

But all was not sweetness and piety in that album. In it, too, were wrenching lyrics reflecting the bitter reality of the ghetto.

> Woman hold her head and cry
> 'Cause her son had been shot down
> On the street and died
> ("Johnny Was")

And, most powerful of all, lyrics that echoed the political warning of the ranking reggae Rastamen:

> That until there are no longer
> First class and second class

Citizens of any nation
Everywhere is war
("War")

These words, if anything, further inflamed the developing political culture, as the tension in the ghetto heightened and the ideological war of the seventies intensified.

For the political reality of life in the Jamaican ghetto was rapidly changing, and for the worse. Added to the inflammatory mix was the influence of the global ideological cold war, introducing a new dimension in Jamaica's politics. Manley and the PNP being in power, the JLP stronghold of Eddie Seaga—Tivoli—came under mounting police pressure. Political tribalism increased sharply; "War" was indeed breaking out in the ghetto. With Manley perceived by the outside world as a new communist threat in a Caribbean already thought to be under the menace of Cuba, the international community began to take a morbid interest in Jamaican politics. We prepared for the *Rastaman Vibration* tour with random violence raging throughout Kingston, exerting much pressure on Bob, who felt close to the two main party enforcers and generals of the streets.

On the heels of this political upheaval came the horse-race doping affair—the "Caymanas" scam—which involved Skill Cole.

Horse racing, always an exciting part of Jamaican life, had become exposed to political corruption, as party enforcers and thugs began to manipulate the outcome of particular races by bribing groom, jockey and trainer, and by doping both horse and rider. Earnings from the racing industry were being used to finance political activity, control of the track on race days being usually under the generalship of the party currently in power. In this context, Skill became involved in a doping episode.

But the horses, for whatever reason, failed to provide the expected results. Many people in the scam did not get paid what they considered their share and, because of the involvement of Skill and his known closeness to Bob, mistakenly linked Bob to the scam. In fact, it was common knowledge that these events were mainly engineered by political ghetto leaders such as Claudie and Tony. However, because of his closeness to Cole, Bob felt obliged to help anyway he could.

Doping problem or no, we had to head for Miami and the National Organization of Record Merchants (NORM) convention, an important occasion for promoting the upcoming album. We left with the doping scandal still raging. After the NORM convention, Bob would work some more on the *Rastaman Vibration* album at the Criteria Recording Studio.

To make this work possible, I had to round up a crew of engineers quickly. I contacted King Sporty, whom I greatly respected and who, when Neville Garrick was jailed in the summer of 1975 for trying to smuggle ganja into Miami on his first trip with the Wailers, had helped bail him out. Sporty, in turn, found Alex Sadkin for us, which was a lucky stroke. Bob developed a great professional respect for Alex, who did a remarkable job on the album, *Rastaman Vibration*, and was later hired by Chris Blackwell. Unhappily, not long after being hired, Alex died in a car crash, leaving both me and Bob with a sense of foreboding.

Rastaman Vibration hit the charts as soon as it was released, adding to Bob's success and his value as a musician.

Success or not, Bob had not abandoned his revolutionary plans. During the two weeks we spent in Miami, he got King Sporty to put him in touch with the Miami-based political dissidents who had fled Jamaica, one of whom was "Schoolboy" (Richard Morrison). It was on this trip, too, that money was funneled to certain individuals to buy what was referred to as "arms."

One day Bob instructed me to give a $40,000 check to someone I knew only as Billy (who is now crippled). To avoid involving me personally, Bob had the check picked up by Yvette Morris for delivery with a letter whose contents none of us knew. Later, as I was going over the bank accounts, I realized that the check had been cashed by a well-known arms dealer.

We returned to Jamaica after completing the album to be once again confronted with the Skill Cole "Caymanas" problem, which had worsened during our absence.

Skill was in deep trouble. The aggrieved parties were so furious that they had kidnapped a jockey involved in the scam. Feelings that the payoff for the fixed double event in the Caymanas scam had been unfair set tempers afire. Since the original deal had been struck at Hope Road among the hangers-on, the unpaid gunmen and enforcers tried to extort repayment of the debt from Bob, who was being asked to shell out two thousand dollars per day. The first payment was extracted from him practically at gunpoint in the ghetto. Finally, Skill fled the island for the USA and ultimately Ethiopia.

To complicate matters, Bob began receiving visits from PNP bad men, who questioned his political allegiance to democratic socialism and Michael Manley. Their suspicion of Bob no doubt sprang from his practice of playing both ends against the middle and using the situation for his own purposes, based on his belief that only a united ghetto could defeat the forces of Babylon.

But the ghetto thugs did not understand this philosophy. They began to question Bob's closeness to people like Claudie

Massop, Seaga's right-hand man. Bob and Skill were often seen hanging out with Massop and his crew at Dizzi Disco, Turntable, and other uptown clubs on Red Hills Road, or visiting the Caymanas Race Track. It was common knowledge that Skill had been part of the racing scam. The suspicion grew that Bob was playing it both ways, in case Manley lost to Seaga.

Given the jittery state of Jamaica's politics in the seventies, we should have seen problems looming.

In the four weeks we had been in Miami, the political climate had become so overheated that on June 19, 1976, the governor general, Sir Florizel Glasspole, declared an island-wide state of emergency based on a charge by the PNP that Seaga and the JLP were plotting with the CIA to discredit the government.

The cauldron was overheating to boiling point, making nonpartisanship impossible. There could be no sitting on the political fence.

Bob, who had come from the PNP side of the ghetto, was now, like everyone else in Jamaica, expected to plainly choose a side.

THE WOMEN

BOB AND RITA

The political and social unrest, however, did not affect Bob's family affairs. Every day Bob had his kids picked up after school and driven to Hope Road. Stevie, Ziggy and Cedella would arrive around two and stay until six or seven o'clock, spending time with their father and watching him play soccer. After the game, he would bundle them off in the VW van to be driven to his house in Bull Bay. With the children gone, he would sit around till eight or nine before venturing out into the Kingston nightlife, very often to Dizzi Disco.

One of the pioneer disco clubs in Kingston, Dizzi was a small club in a cul de sac only two miles from 56 Hope Road. Its entrance was via a short, steep, narrow staircase. It boasted continuously blinking lights against mirrored walls, and featured an intimate dance floor hidden behind beaded curtains. Later I would learn that for Bob, Dizzi's real attraction was Cindy Breakspeare, who worked at the club but was initially cool to Bob's attempts to woo her. The next day, Skill Cole, Bob's constant companion on the excursions, would often render a detailed account of the previous night's courtship.

For my part, I was learning more and more about Bob Marley and beginning to grasp the political and personal context in which he lived. I learned, for example, that Rita Marley and Bob were married in name only. Bob would commonly, during the early period of his career, identify Rita as his sister if questioned by the media. In private, he often reminded Rita that he did not want her using his name. I once witnessed an argument between them on this very subject, during which he reminded her that they were not married under normal circumstances.

He asked, "Rita why you don't stop using my name?" She answered, "But I am married to you," to which he replied, "Rita, how you going on like you don't know how the marriage business go, that my mother was sending for me to come to America and because you have the children, I decided to marry you so that you could get a green card." Often he would add sharply, "Blood claat Rita, don't yuh know dat?"

During one of these family arguments Bob told me that Rita could sign his signature better than he could. I thought this revelation strange but took it as a warning.

One day some money was missing from a Jamaica Citizens Bank account at King Street that Bob maintained jointly with Skill Cole. Thinking that Skill had withdrawn the sum, Bob and I went to the bank and examined the check, which bore what appeared to be his signature. It was then that he blurted out, "Blood claat, Don Taylor, Rita can sign mi name betta dan me!"

Rita was actually treated just like one of the workers. She was paid a salary separate from the household allowance she got to support her and the children. From Bob, Rita received no special treatment. On tour, she was paid like everybody else; at home, she merely hovered in the background.

Rita was raised by a short black woman—barely five feet tall—called Auntie, whom Bob feared. Auntie had a no-nonsense face and a probing way of looking at you that bored deep into your mind.

One time, on a trip to England, Rita was accompanied by Auntie. We were all comfortably ensconced in first class when the stewardess came by with a tray of hors d'oeuvres. Auntie disdained to eat the tidbits, asking me scornfully, "A what dat foolishness dem a serve?" Instead, she began nibbling on doctor fish she had brought aboard in a shut pan. In a blink, the first-class cabin was reeking with the stench of fish, resulting in the abrupt exit of some passengers. No amount of air freshener could get rid of that smell.

According to Bob, Auntie was an obeah woman, a practitioner of this ancient Jamaican religion which, though illegal, still had many followers among the population. Through the years, Auntie continued to live with Rita and have little to do with Bob, although she cared for the children they had together. Bob would often say that he could not make a clean break from Rita because he had been obeahed by Auntie.

In spite the estrangement between Rita and Bob, I soon discovered that a special bond existed between them and learned to stay out of their relationship. On tour, I quickly learned that although they stayed apart in their separate worlds during the day, Bob would often send for Rita as soon as everybody had gone to sleep. Because I had access to Bob's room at all times, I myself regularly observed their nocturnal meetings, which cemented me in my decision to keep out of their private affairs. Never, during Bob's lifetime, did I ever get between them.

Between the first and second tour, Rita got pregnant with Stephanie. Bob never believed the child was his and accused Rita of seeing this other guy. Nevertheless, Rita went ahead and gave the child Bob's surname.

The child, oddly enough, was born with six fingers, and when Bob asked Rita about this peculiarity, she said the trait was inherited from her father, Papa Roy Anderson. Later, Bob met Anderson on the third world tour (Rita had missed the second tour due to pregnancy) at a performance at Stockholm's Tivoli Gardens. Then living in Stockholm, Anderson came backstage to meet Bob, who noticed that his hands were normal. Bob did not ask Rita for an explanation. Instead, he reacted with fiery passion, walking up to her and screaming, "How yu so blood claat lie gal? Yu want a blood claat kick."

After this incident, Bob firmly believed that the child was another man's, and one day he went to Bull Bay to confront the suspected father. After some quick and heated exchanges, with anger blazing and passions boiling, the man stopped Bob dead in his tracks by saying, "Man, I man didn't know she was your wife, 'cause every time I read something, and the I a talk 'bout her, the I seh she is 'im sister.'" The remark suddenly broke the tension between them, and Bob started grinning at his own words, which had come back to haunt him. It was an episode typical of the confusing signals coming from the relationship between Bob and Rita.

Bob's loyalty to Rita, without doubt, was based completely on the fact that she had borne him children. I remember when we were in Germany and one of Bob's baby-mothers, who lived there, came to visit him at the Presidential Suite of the Hamburg Hilton. Obviously irked by the presence of the woman, whose child, Karen, lived in Jamaica, Rita started hassling him about money he was spending on their support. One particular day, the pressure got to be more than Bob could take; he beat Rita mercilessly in the suite, wrecking the room in the process and costing us some large repair bills. We got away lightly only because we were regular guests who usually did not cause trouble.

After settling the bill for damages to the room and boarding the bus, Bob did not take his usual seat in the back. Usually he was the first person on the bus and would sit in the back and meditate. This time, however, he sat in the front with me and told me that he wanted Rita off the tour and sent home right away because she was distracting his concentration. I had never seen him in this mood before; nor did I ever see it again.

The situation was tense enough to require a tactful approach.

I said, "Bob! What is it yu want? Yu want a divorce from Rita? If yu want a divorce, I can handle it, I can get yu a lawyer. But if yu gonna divorce Rita, yu got to cut it off clear! Yu can't be tiptoeing in and out of her room at night when everybody is asleep and gone to bed! Yu got to stop that." Bob flashed his special grin, looked at me, and did an about-face. He replied, "But yu know she is not a bad girl, 'cause I remember the days when she use fi carry mi records on her shoulder, and her shoulder use fi cut from the box of records which she use fi walk wit' through the hot Kingston sun and dirt."

I told him that it looked bad for him to be beating up Rita in front of everyone on the tour. He must have taken my words to heart because, after that conversation he made every effort to control his temper with Rita, and there was never a recurrence of that ugly incident.

I took a cue from that experience and from then on ensured that Rita and the girls occupied a different floor from Bob at different ends of the hotel and either had their own cook or the facilities to cook for themselves. I took the additional precaution of making sure that I was the only person with access to Bob's room.

Out of that brawl also came an agreement for Bob to call Rita, after everyone had settled down for the night, if he needed her. Sometimes they would sit and eat together quietly; sometimes she would come to his room and keep him company. Often she would wash and grease his locks.

It is not commonly understood how important this ritual is to Rastafarians, how they patiently spend hours maintaining the cleanliness of their long hair. Rita would comb Bob's locks late into the night, sometimes even into the early morning hours. To see them lighting up their spliffs during this combing ritual was a beautiful sight, and one I will never forget.

The shifting, unsettled relationship between Bob and Rita sometimes made my life difficult, as did Rita's occasional check-signing. Bob and I had already had a few run-ins with her over this dubious behavior. On one occasion she signed Bob's name to a check for $6,000 from Cayman Music and cashed it.

Bob again warned me, "Yu have to watch Rita Marley, you know, because she can sign my name even better than I can."

In London on our first tour, I got another sample of Rita's dishonesty.

As a token of his appreciation, Bob had decided to divide among everybody on the tour some money he had made on a publishing deal. It was the kind of generous gesture he would make from time to time.

After we had all been paid, Rita and Judy called to say that their share, which they claimed to have put under a mattress, had been stolen by the maid. Bob and I were in the middle of grilling the maid when we grasped that we were victims of another Rita Marley scam. To get a double share of the money, she was even prepared to blame someone innocent. I did not then, and do not now, sit in judgment of Rita. At Bob's hands, she clearly suffered regular mistreatment—including both verbal and physical abuse.

During this time, Bob had accumulated more than thirty million US dollars, and any money that was distributed in his name passed through me. The thirty million was on deposit in three companies—Media Aides, Tuff Gong Records and Bob Marley Music. Allan Cole's name, once on the account, had since been removed. I was the only person who could authorize payment of any kind. In many instances, the banks did not even know Bob. He died with my name still on the accounts.

One day he asked me to go with Rita to look at a house she wanted to buy.

The house, which I will never forget, was in St. Andrew and perched high up in Jacks Hill, two thousand feet above sea level, with a dazzling view of Kingston and the Caribbean. In Jacks Hill, which was a recent suburb, the new and old rich lived cheek-by-jowl. The trip was an eyeopener for me. I never imagined that Jamaicans built and lived in such palatial houses, my own life having kept me scrabbling among the dingy gambling clubs and the recording studios of the plains.

The contrast between the grime of Trench Town and the opulence of this hill was stunning. The house was spread out on two acres of land. It had five bedrooms, a swimming pool, and all the space imaginable for R&R (rest and recreation). Its bathroom faucets were gold plated.

Rita declared that she had found the house she wanted.

I told her I had to first consult Bob and suggested that she take him to look at it.

After the visit, I remember Bob saying to her, "Rita Marley, what's wrong with you, how you like those kind of big life so—you don't realize that the money I have is not my money—is God money! And if you take God money and spend it wrongly and abuse it, God will take it away from yu!"

Bob went on to tell her that he simply could not see himself living in that such a house. Instead, he chose a more moderate residence on Washington Drive in the plains of St. Andrew. Its community was prestigious but understated. Living nearby up the street was Prime Minister Michael Manley. The chosen house was divided into three units, one of which Rita occupied, and Mr. Tseyaye of the Ethiopian Orthodox Church, the other. This hint of a communal yard appealed to Bob's natural instincts.

Though he liked having money, Bob never craved earthly possessions, an attitude that was made even clearer when he toured. That he began and ended every tour with one duffel bag was always a topic of conversation. The shopping sprees indulged in by other members of the touring party were not for Bob.

In contrast to Bob's frugality, I recall querying a bill at a particular hotel in the early days that listed a large charge for "miniatures" and finding out that Rita and the I-Threes had emptied the courtesy bars in their suites. They innocently assumed that the contents of these bars were included in the cost of the room.

Bob always remembered where he came from. He never forgot his faith. Being true believers in the Rasta religion, he and Rita were dedicated to its teachings. But still, they made some slight exceptions from doctrine. For example, Rasta religion demands that children grow locks, but neither Bob nor Rita ever insisted on this observance. Perhaps he recognized that Rasta children still were not completely accepted in Jamaican schools and didn't want to hobble the children with any outward orthodoxy that would hamper their acceptance.

Indeed, it was clear that Bob believed deeply in the advantages of education, for he sent his children to the best private schools (at the time it was Vaz Prep), to which, like all if not most uptowners, they were driven. This arrangement was in place even before he had made a lot of money.

Although Bob had other homes in Jamaica, he spent most of his time at Hope Road. Only rarely did he go to his house in Bull Bay or subsequently to Rita's home on Washington Drive. During the daytime, he was mainly at Hope Road. At night he would either be at Cindy's or at one of his other women.

In an interview given in 1975, he declared his opinion on marriage plainly. "Me never believe in marriage that much. Marriage is a trap to control me; woman is a coward. Man is strong."

This opinion he never hid from Rita, and very often he told her bluntly that she could not walk in Cindy's shoes. Yet when he was asked in 1977 if he would marry Cindy, he answered simply, "She's one of my girlfriends."

Yet though Bob never lived with Rita as man and wife, for some odd reason, it was at her house that he always kept his clothes, as I discovered once when I went to Jamaica to pick up his stuff—at Rita's house. The deep relationship between them was partly grounded in Rita's acceptance of the Rastafarian woman's role and partly in her role as mother of his children.

For whatever else Bob Marley was, he was completely devoted to his children and would frequently remind me that it was because of them that he was working.

9

BOB AND CINDY

That Bob was not a one-woman man was common knowledge. He had converted many highly educated "uptown" women to the ghetto lifestyle, making them into his maids-in-waiting. His converts included lawyers, actresses, oilfield heiresses and top female entertainers, many of whom willingly put their careers on hold to be with Bob. Heading the list was the former Miss World, Cindy Breakspeare.

I had met Cindy years before, when, as manager of Little Anthony and the Imperials, I had brought the group to Jamaica. Cindy was a clerk at our hotel, the Sheraton Kingston, and I recall her having a relationship with Harold Jenkins, a member of Harold Melvin and the Blue Notes, who were with our tour. She had dated Harold in Jamaica and visited him afterwards in Miami while she stayed at Lucien Chen's apartment with her mother. That Harold was just an employee of the Blue Notes and unlikely to be a high flier became a disappointment to Cindy, and the relationship soon fizzled out.

When Bob bought the Hope Road property, in one of life's coincidences, Cindy became his tenant. Before the purchase, both Bob and Cindy had been tenants of Chris Blackwell, each occupying different sides of the house. Bob had made many passes at Cindy, but as far as I know, got nowhere until he became famous and the owner of 56 Hope Road.

With Bob her new landlord, I collected rent from Cindy for the first few months—a minuscule sum of some four hundred dollars. One day, when I went to collect the monthly rent, Cindy told me that she had already paid Bob. I should have deduced then that something was developing between them, but I missed the signs. Nor did I ask Bob about the rent payment, probably because the amount of money was so small. But it was then that I began suspecting that a relationship was unfolding between them.

I also remembered the stories Skill used to tell about the visits he and Bob made to Cindy at Dizzi Disco where she worked. Bob had been sending signals to her even when Cindy was still Chris Blackwell's tenant. But his efforts bore fruit only after Bob had bought the Hope Road house from Blackwell.

A serious relationship was developing between them—that was made clear to me one night when I called Bob as I was about to take my second wife, Apryl, to the movies. Bob asked me to come and pick him up and, uncharacteristically, brought Cindy with him (Bob did not take women to movies). Nevertheless, I was still taken aback when Cindy entered the Miss World contest, and Bob asked me to pay her way to London and arrange the details of her trip.

At that time in Jamaica, the socialist Manley regime abhorred the once government-endorsed beauty contests. Black-power consciousness being the order of the day, Manley's government had come out against beauty contests, feeling that this was no time for the marketing of female flesh.

Cindy's entry in the Miss World contest and Bob's support of her could easily have proven embarrassing to him, as his fans expected him to be in tune with the trends of the time.

For its part, the government gave neither sympathy nor support to any beauty contest entrant from Jamaica, and the private sector, fearful of bucking the official position, also fell in line, reducing the level of funding for Jamaica's participation in the Miss World finals. Only the governor general, Sir Florizel Glasspole, seemed enthusiastic about the beauties. This opposition meant that Cindy, as Miss Jamaica, had little or no support—monetary or otherwise.

Acting on Bob's instructions, I transferred thousands of pounds for Cindy's expenses and arranged for the money to be disbursed through our public-relations agency. (Later, this transaction would lead to rumors that Cindy had bought the crown.)

Such a burst of generosity was not usual for Bob, but I still did not take his relationship with Cindy seriously. He was already, at the time, openly going about with two other friends of Cindy's, Virginia Burke and her sister, Nancy. In fact, I was told that Bob—typically—was sleeping with both of them as well as with Cindy.

In helping Bob with his personal life I only did what he asked. Later, I never discussed with him his feelings about Cindy's pregnancy or the birth of their son, Damien. All I knew what that Bob loved to have children. Indeed, he loved all children. One of his habits on tour was to make impromptu stops, get out of the car and mix with the people, especially the children. He once said, "Children are wonderful. It don't take plenty y'know. Just a nice girl who don't take birth control. Sexual intercourse is a lovely thing."

Bob cared for Cindy—that was obvious. I remember when we were working on the *Kaya* album and staying at 1 Harrington Gardens in London, Cindy came to stay with Bob. On one particular night while Cindy and Bob were cooling out in his room, some ladies dropped by to visit him, and he told me to have them wait in my room on the first floor. Fifteen minutes later, Bob came down to meet his female fans, leaving Cindy alone in his apartment. Soon Cindy came looking for him and caught him sitting close to one of the women. Irritated, she snapped that if he was going to behave that way, she was leaving, and turned on her heels and walked away. (This incident took place after Bob's alleged affairs with Nancy Burke and her sister.) Bob shouted at me to go and bring her back, but I was too slow to react. He jumped up and went after her himself—the first time I had ever seen Bob actually pursue a woman.

I watched as he persuaded her to return upstairs to his apartment. A few hours later, I went to check on him, and finding Cindy there, said offhandedly to her, "Boy, Bob must really love you to chase after you so," which irritated her. That was when it dawned on me just how much Bob really loved Cindy.

The following day when I saw Bob I took a "jive" and said, "Bob, I didn't know yuh got it so bad that yuh told Cindy how much yuh love her and would do anything for her." He replied, "Don Taylor, what would you do in an intimate situation if while you are on the upstroke a woman look you in the eye and ask if you love her?"

The only woman Bob loved, and the only one who had any kind of leverage over him—it became clear to me after that—was Cindy. But as Cindy's power over him grew, so did Bob's gradual withdrawal. He said to me once, "When you money done you ain't got no friends" (he loved to hear Billie Holiday

Maximum dread—Bob in terrifying mood. (© Retna Pictures)

Above: Bob's wife, Rita Marley.
Opposite: Ethnic peoples everywhere hailed Bob as a saviour.

A heartbreaking shot taken of Bob in Paris shortly before his death. (© Rex Features)

Island Records boss, Chris Blackwell. (© Camera Press)

Father and son. Ziggy Marley (inset) is carrying on his father's glorious tradition.

Happy days—as we all love to remember him.

sing "God Bless the Child," which contains this sentiment). "If the money done, you may not have a woman either."

Reflecting on their relationship, I now believe that Cindy, beset by Bob's involvement with many women as well as by his paper marriage to Rita, probably decided it was in her best interest to get pregnant. She probably felt, I have always thought, that pregnancy would give her situation stability and protect her in a crisis—whether financial or physical.

And Bob did help her, financially and otherwise. For instance, when Cindy came up with the idea for her company, Ital Craft, Bob instructed me to supply her with $100,000 start-up capital. When Cindy needed some beads for her business, Bob bought them in Australia while he was on tour, and Rita herself lugged them to Jamaica.

After Cindy became pregnant, I received a call from Bob while I was in Miami. He told me that some insurance guy named Chunky Lopez was migrating and selling his house in Cherry Gardens, one of the more exclusive residential areas in Kingston. He instructed me to buy the house for Cindy and the baby. I did as he instructed, paying the guy US$49,000 for the house, into which Cindy moved. She lived there until her marriage to Tom Tavares Finson.

All these events reaffirmed my earlier belief that Cindy cleverly timed her relationship with Bob for her own personal betterment. It was all very simple: Bob had become big; he could and would do anything for her.

On winning the Miss World beauty contest, she took the opportunity to publicly declare that Bob Marley was her man and that she wanted to hurry home to her Rasta. I still believe that her well-timed revelation was a deliberate strategy to prop up their affair, which had so far been secret, by announcing it to the world. In fact, the declaration created quite a stir among

Bob's crowd. Soon afterwards, Cindy became pregnant and thus ensured a steady supply of money from Bob.

Before Bob bought her the house in Cherry Gardens, Cindy had never lived in such grand style, her family having fallen on hard times when she was very young. Bob might well have told Cindy that he intended to marry her and that his marriage to Rita was only a convenience. But to my mind, Cindy's tolerance of Bob's continued intimate associations with her friends, spoke volumes about her real intentions.

Indeed, Cindy somewhat shocked me, perhaps because I had always naively thought that upper-class Jamaican women were raised to have morals. But when I found out that Cindy knew her friends were sleeping with Bob yet closed her eyes to his flings, I lost all respect for her. Virginia Burke, for instance, started seeing Allan Cole even though she knew that he was also going with Judy Mowatt.

But none of these goings-on in any way affected the closeness between Bob and Cindy, and their relationship continued just as intensely after their son, Damien, was born.

One consequence of this relationship was that the Rastas began accusing Bob of moving into uptown society, creating rumblings and discontent in the very quarters from which his music had sprung. For a while, these charges certainly panicked all of us business people. To the ghetto, Bob was beginning to look like a sellout, especially since he was a militant who sang and talked about black and Rasta unity. Indeed, the downtown people always interpreted his protest music as speaking especially for them. So with the talk that Bob was dating Cindy and moving into uptown society, the Rastas and other militant brethren began to question his association with these white girls, especially in Jamaica. Bob's answer to the Rasta community was, "Wha' happen to my brothers and sisters, yu no see me a carry Rasta uptown?" That reply silenced his critics. He was never questioned again.

What the ghetto people failed to appreciate was that Bob, like any other successful businessman, had groomed himself and was now moving in a social level where everyone looked out for his own best interest. He was continually mixing with kings and queens. He was dating princesses, being entertained by their fathers, and becoming exposed to what he regarded as a corrupt way of life.

As Bob moved up the social ladder, he was introduced to many of the upscale crowd's bad habits, including cocaine. At the end of his career, around the time of his death, a scandal was raging about his alleged cocaine use. But I, who was constantly at his side, saw no evidence that Bob used cocaine. Ziggy told Rita and me that one day he saw his dad put a white powder up his nose and asked what it was. His father replied that the substance was crushed aspirin. But I, Don Taylor, never saw Bob use cocaine and would have hard time believing that he ever had. If Bob ever used cocaine, he had to be under someone's influence.

Bob Marley was three distinct persons in one—that I learned from his relationship with Cindy.

The first was Bob Marley the revolutionary, the "Tuff Gong."

The second was Robert Nesta Marley, an understanding, meek and kind human being who loved Cindy and his children and who would listen with understanding to anyone's problems.

The third was Bob Marley, reggae superstar and musical genius par excellence.

This, then, was the complex picture of Bob Marley—public and private—that emerged as we approached the final days of 1976.

POLITRICKS

10

THE FREE CONCERT AND THE ASSASSINATION ATTEMPT

I had been dividing my time—during this period—between Miami and Kingston. In November of 1976, I flew in to Jamaica to handle some personal business as well as Bob's management portfolio. For rest and relaxation I planned to hang out at two gambling clubs, Norman's and House of Chen, both offshoots of another club that had been near to Dizzi, the disco Bob used to frequent.

At these clubs, games of chance such as poker, craps or Mah Jong (at all of which I was pretty adept) would commonly continue nonstop for days and nights, with millions routinely won and lost. There the real Jamaican gamblers would mingle, sated with all the whisky and food they could consume.

Christmas was approaching, a more magical season in Jamaica than in many developed countries of the world. Traditionally, the celebrations of Christmas in Jamaica begin as early as October. Nature herself seems to participate in the revelries by bedecking the land in a profusion of red, pink and white poinsettias. Merrymakers would sometimes make the rounds of six or more office and private parties in an evening that would stretch into the wee hours of the morning.

In between partying and attending to my own personal business, I visited Bob at Hope Road to find out what he had in mind for Christmas.

Even by Jamaican standards, it was a time of unprecedented violence and mayhem. Michael Manley had lately imposed a state of emergency on the country. Fresh in the news was a grisly incident known as the Green Bay Massacre, where ten youths had been lured to their deaths by the army and massacred in cold blood on the Hellshire hills. The country later learned that an entire cadre of PNP bad men, following false leads about where they could pick up guns for an anti-JLP raid, had walked into an army ambush. It was a chilling incident, and the kind one could hardly believe would ever happen in Jamaica. Civil war seemed imminent.

The economy had deteriorated rapidly; the treasury was broke; Jamaica had stumbled badly since the heady first days of Independence.

The ghettos had become "hot." A disastrous fire with political implications had occurred on Orange Street. As Bob said in June of 1976, "We trying to make things easier but y'know, the politics keep its teeth. You have two parties fighting each other so we come like nutten because them guys always fighting and claiming to be the big guys. Plenty people fight for jobs, so the only way to get a job is to be on one side or the other, otherwise you suffer, you suffer and they hurt you bad. They burn houses with people in it, babies in it, in Jamaica, you know. I don't really understand it bwoy, really can't understand that. And I know it is politicians doing it. It's the youth that catches the place afire, but it is the politicians influence. That really not look good. Politics, man."

The conflict had escalated beyond imagination as larger and larger areas of Kingston became politically tribalized and under the rule of leading gangs of either party. The walls of the ghettos were scribbled with menacing graffiti: "PNP enter at own risk"; "JLP keep out—or death."

Ulysses Estrada, the Cuban ambassador, was heard to threaten Jamaicans with consequences if they interfered with the "revolution." No one knew whether he was referring to the Cuban or the Jamaican revolution.

Prime Minister Manley bluntly urged Jamaicans who wished to become rich to leave on one of the "five flights a day to Miami." The newly emerged middle class, the business trained, both of whom are indispensable to any country, took him at his word and began an exodus to the USA and UK. Many settled in Miami, depriving Jamaica of its best and brightest entrepreneurs and workers. In the panic, many of those fleeing sold their houses for whatever little price in US dollars they could get. Some simply walked away, abandoning the houses to the banks and insurance companies. Foreign exchange poured out of the country in illegal transfers.

The ideological conflict between the Manley/Seaga factions was raging out of control. To say that Jamaica was convulsed by the turmoil of revolution would not have been an overstatement. The ghettos, split into warring political parties, were at boiling point.

It was against this context that Bob felt he wanted to stage a show in Jamaica for Christmas, a Christmas morning show to be exact. I saw his idea as a good money-earner as well as an opportunity to lift the spirits of the embattled, politically weary people.

A concert would fit right in with the traditional Jamaican merrymaking at Christmas, which has always been celebrated with any number of shows. I cherished boyhood memories of dressing up in new clothes and, on Christmas morning, attending a concert followed by a stroll along downtown King Street, where everyone joined in the fun and frolic of street-side vending. These happy memories were of a time long before the neglect of Kingston and the vicious eruption of partisan violence.

I had assumed that Bob had in mind a paying concert, but he quickly dispelled this notion. He said, "Yu blood claat mad, yu would a mash up everybody business, yu woudda tek weh the little man food. We nuh need nuh more money out of we Jamaican people." Bob simply refused to make money out of the poor by charging admission to the concert. His own concert, being free, would contrast sharply with the trend of commercial Christmas stage shows that had become as ubiquitous in Jamaica as plum pudding and sorrel and that were staged from one end of the island to the other.

Bob's reasoning was simple: Jamaicans had been good to him; in this time of turmoil and divisiveness, he felt a need to do something to relieve the pressure on the people. I heartily agreed with his thinking. Bob and his musical accomplishments were, at the time, the only really good news coming out of Jamaica. He had become a symbol of hope and escape to the downtrodden.

Sitting on the verandah, Bob suggested that the concert be called the "Smile Jamaica" concert. He had penned these lyrics on that theme:

> Help my people help them right
> O Lord help us tonight
> Cast away the evil spell
> Pour some water in the well

Where would the concert be held? Bob wanted the venue

to be a place where the rich, the poor and the middle class could mingle without tension. I suggested as a site the grounds of Jamaica House, location of the prime minister's office and only a stone's throw away from Hope Road.

Originally designed to be the official residence of the prime minister, Jamaica House, built in 1963, was meant to be the Jamaican equivalent of the White House and 10 Downing Street. But it had seldom served as the official residence of the head of government. Sir Alexander Bustamante had occupied it only briefly just before retiring as the first prime minister of an independent Jamaica. Hugh Shearer, a bachelor who took over as prime minister from Sir Donald Sangster (who died only a few weeks after winning the general elections of 1967), had no use for such an enormous house. When Michael Manley assumed office in 1972, he converted Jamaica House from a residence into the office of the prime minister.

With its vast grounds, Jamaica House struck me as the perfect venue for Bob's idea of a concert appealing to all the people. Located midway between the neighborhoods of the haves and the have-nots, it was a site guaranteed to make everyone feel safe and protected.

Bob liked the idea so much that he picked up the phone, called the prime minister, and was immediately put through— an indication of his power. In fact, Bob and Manley had grown close over the years. Manley never hid his admiration for Bob's musical achievements and had written many pieces on reggae music and its global cultural impact.

The prime minister responded with great enthusiasm and invited Bob to come Jamaica House immediately for a discussion. We were admitted by the guards at the gate without hesitation and drove up the impressive driveway past the expansive lawn. We climbed the semicircular staircase to the prime minister's office, which was guarded by charming secretaries, the prime minister's personal assistant, as well as security men who discreetly observed us from a distance.

Anxiously awaiting our arrival, Manley, who virtually greeted us at the door, was his usual impressive self, his six-foot stature clad in a hallmark Kareeba suit, his hair graying at the temples, his manner oozing the kind of charm usually reserved for the stage. As he focused all his geniality on me, a stranger he was meeting for the first time, Manley was not only self-possessed and confident, he also radiated a hint of mischief. This must be what they call charisma, I thought to myself, feeling like a long-lost brothers.

He asked Bob how his career was going and spoke briefly about the problems ravaging the country and how this gesture by Bob would help ease the tensions. Bob explained that he did not want the concert to be politicized, repeating himself to emphasize this point.

The prime minister then had his secretary call his minister of state, Senator Arnold Bertram, whom I had only heard of through press reports. Bertram arrived, was introduced, listened to our proposal, and then invited us to adjourn to his office—a trailer-like building across the lawn erected during the conversion of Jamaica House into prime minister's office. Bob again emphasized the unifying intent of the concert and his wish for all Jamaica to share equally in a nonpartisan celebration.

The preliminary details settled, Bob and I called a press conference at Hope Road to announce the concert, billing it as a joint production by Bob Marley and the government.

Almost immediately afterwards, with timing that struck me as hurried and contrived, the government announced the date of the next general election. The die was cast, and the vibes became sinister, as if a dark cloud had suddenly descended over the island and the concert. People around Bob became edgy and concerned.

We did not know then that that the cold war had come to Jamaica, that our small island had become one of its flash points, that Jamaica was being manipulated to further the ideological ends of opposing global powers. Between the political factions among us, a yawning gulf had opened. Stoked by outside influences, political tribalization on the island was goaded to extremism. No longer was the game played locally and solely between JLP and PNP. The major players were now East and West (Russia and Cuba vs. USA, symbolized in the rivalry between East Kingston and West Kingston). With the revelations of the role Noriega and Panama played in events then boiling in the Caribbean, the factionalism of those hot-blooded days, in hindsight, now take on a sinister appearance. Not in our wildest nightmares did we think that the CIA would traffic in drugs and then funnel the ill-gotten profits to selected Jamaican partisans.

JLP operatives around Bob—Claudie Massop, Tommy Cowan, Harry J and Tek Life—all warned him that their party did not want his free concert. Claudie, who was then in prison, sent Bob an urgent message to this effect.

The JLP saw the concert as an endorsement of Michael Manley and his socialist policies and took it as a slap in the face. They felt vehemently that the state of emergency had been trumped up only for the purpose of discrediting their party, a view later accepted by an independent inquiry.

In face of the JLP's opposition, a compromise agreement was struck to move the concert from Jamaica House to National Heroes Circle. Staging the concert at Jamaica House, it was felt, would imply support for the PNP, whose "bad men," through Tony Welch, had made it clear that they strongly supported the original venue. National Heroes Circle having been established as a graveyard for Jamaican heroes by a previous JLP government, and being the site of a monument to Marcus Mosiah Garvey, seemed to be symbolically neutral ground.

The cauldron, however, continued to boil, especially as the PNP hailed the concert as a grand gesture and strongly voiced their support of it. Even among our immediate circle, there was resentment. I clearly remember that Judy Mowatt opposed the concert because she did not want to be affiliated, even by implication, to any political group.

Meanwhile, I was trying my best to keep the boat upright, while steering through the rough waters.

We began the rehearsing. Sparks continued to fly in many quarters. A feverish tension mounted, and the pressure built up as we discovered daily, if not hourly, the profound partisan feelings people had about the concert. I kept working to convince Judy to participate, arranging meetings with her in an attempt to win her over, but always coming away convinced that she would not budge.

Messages poured in from both sides. JLP emissaries kept telling us that "Seaga say this" or "Seaga say that." But Bob didn't seem to care nor to take these messages seriously. His usual reply that he did not accept messages from any messenger boy, that if Seaga had something to say, "Him have to say it to me direct."

Ignoring the confusion, I began releasing funds to pay for the concert, whose costs were being underwritten entirely by Bob. I went to the USA to hire a crew to film it. Everything would be done exactly right. Even though the concert was free, there would be no corners cut or expense spared.

When I returned from New York, I went to see Bob, who described an unsettling incident that had occurred in my absence. He told me, "Don Taylor, when you were not here, the other day a white boy came here and told me that if I do not tone down my blood claat lyrics and if me no stop tek weh the white people them from America them a go tek weh me visa and me can't go to America again." I asked Bob what he had said to the man. He said, "I told him tek yu blood claat out of my yard, before me lick yu up." Bob had been surrounded by his men with their guns. He said, "You should see the white man run out of Hope Road like a madman into his car and speed away."

The US, at that time squarely behind Seaga and the JLP, frowned on Bob's close association with Michael Manley, whose own friendship with Fidel Castro was regarded as disturbing as Bob's strong appeal to white American youths. After hearing Bob describe the incident, I knew immediately, based on my US army experience, that his visitor had been a CIA agent.

As Bob was undeterred and still resolved to hold the concert, I wired my standby crew in America, confirming the arrangements I had made with them in New York.

Normal life prevailed outside of the tense inner circle of the Wailers, where arguments continued to periodically rage for or against the concert. For my personal relaxation, I continued visiting the gambling clubs.

I was in the middle of a game when I had to leave to go to Miami to pick up a $143,000 check for Bob. I also had arranged to meet with Chris Blackwell, who was in Jamaica at the Sheraton in New Kingston, and to pick him up and take him to the concert rehearsals at Hope Road. Relinquishing my hand to a friend, Dynamite Lyn, to play for me while I tended to business, I flew off to Miami that morning.

On my return the following day, I drove my rented car straight from the airport to the club to find that Dynamite had done considerably better than the sixty thousand dollars I had been losing at my departure and was now breaking even. I ate a satisfying curry goat dinner at the House of Chen before driving to the Sheraton Hotel to pick up Chris. But Chris, it turned out, had already left.

I proceeded straight to 56 Hope Road. In the car I still had a couple cases of whisky I had bought earlier and a briefcase purchased in Miami for a friend. I also had on me the royalty check for $143,000 that I had brought back for Bob.

I parked the car as usual under the driving alcove of 56 Hope Road and entered the house through the front door. Hearing the rehearsal in progress, I peeked into the music room located downstairs next to the kitchen. The full band was at work, but Bob was missing. I found him standing in the corner of the kitchen cutting a grapefruit.

I told him I wanted to speak with him and that I would also like a piece of grapefruit. He beckoned me to come and get it. Just then, as I reached for the grapefruit, I heard a sound like firecrackers. It was Christmas in Jamaica. Firecrackers at this time of the year are a common background noise. I paid little attention. Bob, however, looked startled and asked, "Who the blood claat a bus firecracker in mi yard?"

Before he could finish the sentence, the kitchen was shattered by an ominous and repetitious "rat-ta-tat, rat-ta-tat" sound. Suddenly, I felt a strange burning sensation, and even before I realized that I had been shot, my body went limp and I pitched forward on to Bob, whose only exclamation was, "Selassie I Jah Rastafari."

I recall Bob holding me up in front of him while the shooting continued. When the hail of fire had finally stopped, he let me go, and I tumbled onto the floor, unconscious. Everything had happened as if in a dream.

I regained consciousness and found myself crumpled on the floor of the kitchen, amid a ghastly silence. Gradually I could hear quarreling voices. I heard Bob say, "They shoot up Don Taylor, Don Taylor dead or something." The Rastafarians were arguing and refusing to lift me up off the floor because they objected to handling "deaders." I tried to say something but could not speak. A great sense of shock, of amusing reality, swept over me in an absurd wave.

I did not know it then, but my aorta had been punctured. I was rapidly losing blood.

In the shock, I felt as if my consciousness had been split into two separate parts: one hovered in the air, heard and understood everything but was detached from all pain and suffering; the other was crammed inside the riddled body lying on the kitchen floor and struggling through the mist of consciousness to find out how badly it was hurt. The hovering consciousness whispered that maybe my "joint" (penis) had been shot off. On the floor, the wounded body slowly pushed its hand into its waist to assure that its joint was still intact before slumping again into unconsciousness.

Bob and the police lifted me up from the floor and put me in the backseat of the police car. I heard one of the policemen mumble crossly, "Damn, you know mi siren don't work!" a comment I found quite amusing.

I also heard a policeman say that I had been shot in the abdomen and needed immediate medical attention. Another police vehicle with a siren pulled into the driveway and escorted us to the University Hospital, not far from 56 Hope Road.

Still not able to see or speak, I could, nevertheless, hear everything. I overheard a nurse saying she needed two stretchers as one of the victims was dead, but did not think for a second that she meant me. Obviously, I was not dead. Indeed, my senses were functioning clearly. I could hear everything.

The stretchers having arrived, the nurse checked me briskly and pronounced, "This one is dead, put him in the metal stretcher, and take that one over there"—meaning Bob. Both parts of my consciousness tried to scream, "No, I am alive!" But no sound issued from the torn body bleeding helplessly on the stretcher. It occurred to me, as my hovering self whispered ominously, that I might be buried alive.

I heard the nurse tell the orderly to wheel me to the door of the morgue where the doctor could pronounce me dead before I was tagged. As an orderly began pushing me down the corridor to the morgue, I heard in the background another voice, this one with a Bahamian lilt and an edge of authority that sounded like it belonged to a doctor, ask about my condition. Both my selves begged him silently to take a look, tried to cry out aloud to him but couldn't. When the orderly explained that he intended deposit me beside the door of the morgue, the doctor said, to my relief, "Let me check him first before you take him to the morgue." Later I learned that the voice belonged to an intern, Dr. Phillip Thompson.

The doctor approached the stretcher; I felt his touch; I heard him gasp, "This man is not dead, he is alive."

Jolted by an electric charge of relief and excitement, I was wheeled back into the emergency room under urgent doctor's orders to be immediately given a blood transfusion. But this was Christmas, and in an incident typical of Jamaica in the seventies, the lady with the only key to the blood bank was away at a party. She turned out to be a Mrs. Trought, wife of the deputy commissioner of police, Larry Trought, the prime minister's chief man who had himself played an important part in the state of emergency. He was also someone I had known from the days of my youth and whom I always called "godfather," as a term of respect.

The consciousness in the body sprawled on the stretcher tried to smile feebly at this turn of events. Manley's experiments in socialism and the resulting decline in the economy had so strapped all Jamaican hospitals that everyone had heard tales of this kind about the ludicrous shortages. The hospitals were in such a pitiful state that patients often had to supply their own food and blankets. And here I was, on a stretcher and bleeding to death, experiencing the desperate shortages firsthand.

Finally the doctor was able to get me stabilized, and I regained consciousness. I opened my eyes, the two parts of my consciousness united, and a burning pain blasted through my body as if someone had rubbed pepper in my wounds. Standing over me were Prime Minister Michael Manley and his wife Beverly, who was weeping. I do not recall what they said, but I could see the concern in their eyes.

It asked about Bob and was told that he had been shot through the arm and nicked in the chest. Rita, I was told, had been shot in her head, between scalp and skull. She underwent surgery for the removal of the bullet and was treated and released. I was the most seriously wounded and needed an immediate operation to assess the extent of the internal damage.

I was still so excited at being alive that, when it was time for the operation, I forgot to tell the doctor or the nurses (and they forgot to ask) about the curry goat dinner I had eaten earlier at the House of Chen.

The operation was as successful as it could have been, and I awoke in the recovery room. Groggy from the anesthesia as I lay on a gurney, I regurgitated the curry goat dinner and began to suffocate on the food. But once again fate played its hand; the doctor, having forgotten his bag in the recovery room, returned just in time to take corrective action.

The next morning, I woke in the recovery room of the University Hospital with a bullet still lodged in my spine. Both my left and right sides were paralyzed. I couldn't move an inch. I asked Doctor Thompson why he did not operate and remove the bullet. He replied that it was a miracle I was still alive and should consider myself lucky even with the loss of sensation in my sides. To me his answer sounded like an excuse: obviously the hospital was not equipped to treat my type of gunshot wound.

My friends, by this time, had got in touch with my second wife, Apryl Beckford-Taylor, who was then nine months pregnant with my son Christopher. She flew down from Miami as soon as she learned of the shooting.

I asked her to contact the US Veterans Administration, inform them of my military service and get from them the names of VA doctors experienced in treating bullet wounds. Through the Veterans Administration in Miami, we were put in touch with Dr. William Bacon. Chris Blackwell paid for my transfer to Miami by a chartered medical plane. A two-hour operation was performed on my spine at the Cedars of Lebanon Hospital, and by the next morning I was walking around the hospital.

I remained in Miami convalescing at my house in the south-west area, a far cry from the overtown slums where I lived when I had first arrived from Jamaica.

In spite of the shooting, or perhaps because of it, many people felt that, if only as a symbolic gesture against the raging gun violence in Jamaica, the show should go on as planned. Prime Minister Manley strongly urged Bob to perform. The concert would now feature Third World, and I later learned that as tributes to Bob poured in on the radio, he wavered in his decision until Tony Spaulding finally convinced him to appear on stage.

Word that Bob had decided to perform spread like wildfire—band members Kinsey, Downie and Carly were located, and Cat Coore chosen to fill in for Family Man, who could not be reached.

Bob bounded onto the stage and by all reports gave a superlative performance. He spoke to the crowd, saying, "When mi decide to do dis ya concert two an a half months ago, me was told dere was no politics, I just wanted to play fe de love of the people," and then broke into "War":

> That until the basic human rights
> are equally guaranteed to all
> Everywhere is war.

After the concert Bob went to his house in Nassau to rest, taking with him Rita and all the kids, his as well as hers. We kept in touch by telephone, discussing business and inquiring after each other's health. We talked about an invitation we had received, through Tony Spaulding, from Fidel Castro, to come and convalesce in the safety of Cuba.

As a sequel, I would later find out that among the crew hired to come to Jamaica was the son of a prominent CIA official who had traveled under an alias. This information convinced me that the CIA had been behind the plot to kill Bob Marley because of his possible influence on Jamaican politics and on the wider world. I also learned that about fifty-six bullets had been fired at Bob but, except for the nick in his chest, none had really hit him. I still vividly remember his heartfelt cry of "Selassie I Jah Rastafari" as the bullets flew around us, spraying the kitchen.

I also learned from Bob that he had told the police that he could prove who had shot him. He also prophesied that the same number of bullets fired at him would one day cut down his attacker. Street myth has it that Claudie Massop, who was subsequently killed by the police, was riddled with fifty-six bullets.

Indeed, suspicion of involvement in the attempted assassination soon fell on the Massop camp, prompting me to recall a visit by Stewbert, a Tony Welch accomplice, to the Hope Road house a few days before the attempted assassination. Stewbert said he had come hoping to speak to Bob. Standing on the verandah, he had asked me, with a serious look, whether I carried a gun. I asked him why I would need a gun with someone like him around. Later, we would learn that Stewbert had just been recently released from prison. Had he come to the house with instructions to warn us?

I also later heard that the gunmen thought they had killed Bob and that it was probably the shield of my body that had saved his life. I didn't see the gunmen. My back had been turned to the door. I only felt and heard the shooting. But, of course, I'll never forget it.

I still have a bullet lodged in my left thigh, and when the weather is cold or I'm very tired, it makes me limp.

11
THE AFTERMATH

Two weeks after my Miami operation, while I was still walking with a cane, Bob asked me to come to the Bahamas and visit him at Chris Blackwell's house on the western side of Nassau, where he had been staying. The dust on the assassination had settled, and we needed to resume his career. In the planning stage was a trip to London to cut some albums. I asked him to pick me up at the Nassau airport, but when I landed, there was a message at the airline telling to take a cab.

Arriving at the house, I found that Bob had gone to Joe Stebleski's hotel. On his return, he explained that four thousand dollars was missing from a bag he kept under his bed and, because he was upset over the loss, he hadn't been able to meet me at the airport. His suspicion had fallen on Joe Stebleski, who had been hanging around, trying to ingratiate himself with Bob.

Despite the turmoil of the previous weeks, Bob's domestic scene was ever the same.

Bob called in his daughter, Cedella, and questioned her about whether Rita had ever sent her to get his bag. Despite all his probing, however, the mystery of the disappearing money was never solved and eventually just dropped. There was never any real evidence, then or now, that either Stebleski, Rita, or Cedella had stolen the money.

The next few days Bob spent planning future tours, records and concerts. Occasionally, he would break away and take Chris's boat far out to sea. While his companions fished, he would enjoy a spliff, meditate, and jot down outlines of songs he planned to use on the *Kaya* album.

For some three years now, I had had been managing Bob with nothing between us but a gentlemen's agreement. Not until November of 1976 did Bob actually confirm in the following letter that I was authorized to act as his agent, and David Steinberg as his attorney.

19 November 1976

Mr. Oscar Cohen
Associated Booking Corporation
445 Park Avenue
New York, NY 10022

Dear Mr. Cohen:

Please be advised that Don Taylor and David J. Steinberg, Esq. still represent me in the capacity of Personal Manager and Attorney respectively.

Therefore, any matters with regard to my interests may be handled by them along the lines of their employ.

Yours very truly

Robert Marley

Following our meetings in Nassau, Bob and I agreed to leave for London in January 1977, and I made travel arrangements for the band. *Exodus*, the album we had just released, had stayed on the British charts for fifty-six weeks. In the wake of its success and hype, Bob began planning two follow-up albums, *Kaya* and *Survival*.

Our band now consisted of Alvin "Seco" Patterson, Carly and Aston "Family Man" Barrett, and Tyrone "Organ D' Downie. Donald Kinsey had been so spooked by the assassination attempt that he decided not to accompany us, and we landed in London without a guitarist. Eventually, we hired Junior Marvin as a session musician. Other personnel, such as the I-Threes, Bob decided to fly in as needed to lay down the tracks.

With our arrival in London, Bob settled down immediately into a satisfying routine at an Oakley Street apartment (he had asked to be as close as possible to Battersea Park, where he could indulge his other passion—soccer). He seemed to radiate a calm and mellow mood. His apartment had its own private entry separate from the one used by band members. He had hired Lucky Gordon (of Christine Keeler fame) as his personal cook. To allow Bob privacy, I myself had taken an apartment at No. 1 Harrington Gardens.

From the early afternoon, say 3 p.m. until the early morning, Bob would work in the studio. Between 10 a.m. and noon he played soccer. He also took time to mingle with other musicians such as the Clash, who were emerging on the London scene.

Bob was clearly entering an interlude of calmness marked by a love of life and a love for all the special women, both past and present, around him.

On the one hand, there were his old familiar loves such as Cindy, Virginia Burke and her sister Nancy; on the other hand, there was also an exciting new love, the strikingly beautiful Princess Yashi.

Yashi was a young woman of money and class—a slim Arab beauty, five feet seven inches tall, with a smooth olive complexion and the gait of a thoroughbred. Daughter of the oil minister of Libya, Yashi walked with assurance and purpose. Her smile lit up every corner of her face, and the twinkle in her dark eyes suggested the laughter of a bygone era of feminine conquest, a Delilah seeking her Samson.

Yashi, who had just started boarding school in London, was reveling in her freedom, although as the daughter of the Libyan oil minister, she was somewhat restricted by her bodyguards. It was Yashi who made Bob buy the only suit I have ever known him to own. He was taking her to Tramps, then the most fashionable nightclub in London, and felt he needed to wear a suit and tie. The following day, when I saw him, he was on an unusual high, the effect of four bottles of Dom Perignon champagne, two of which had been a gift from the club. These details he recounted to me the morning after, still dressed in the suit in which he had slept that night. I never saw him in a suit again.

Bob and Yashi soon became a hot item on the London scene, where he was her constant escort.

Once when Yashi visited Bob in Miami, we went to dinner at the Forge on 79th Street. Yashi, who drank only the best wines, ordered her favorite, a 1953 Chateau Lafite Rothschild, racking up a bill for thirty-five thousand dollars. Bob glanced at it, handed it to me and told me to put it on my American Express card.

"Do you know how much this is?" I asked him. Bob replied, "Nuh, three thousand five hundred dollars." I said, "No, Bob, is thirty-five thousand dollars." He exclaimed, "What!" and beckoned to me and the waiter to follow him outside. Out of earshot and sight of Yashi, he said to the waiter, "Nuh, mistake you mek?" The waiter replied, "No, Mr. Marley, that's the price." Bob pressed, "Then 'ow yu know mi could a pay the bill?" to which the maitre d', in the usual pompous voice of his trade, shot back, "Mr. Marley, we know who you are, and your credit is always good." It was a fitting ending to an enjoyable evening.

In spite of the presence of Yashi in London, Bob still loved to have as many women around him as he could get, so he sent for Cindy to join him. He had by now become even more mellow and totally absorbed in the London life. The trauma of the shooting incident now seemed squarely behind him as he moved into a whole new plateau of creativity.

With his thoughts on love, Bob was inspired to write such songs as "Is This Love," and most of the other love songs in the *Kaya* album.

It was during this period that I also saw for myself his memorable way of song writing.

Bob would begin by picking out a rhythm on his guitar in the studio. Carly and Family Man would then come in, establish the rhythm, and Bob would lay down the lyrics from his head. I have often wondered why he used this method of composing and how he was able to write without taping his lyrics. But I think that bitter lessons learned from Sims, Nash and Chris Blackwell had led him, in self-protection, to this odd system. Perhaps his inherent mistrust of the music scene was one compelling reason why he never wrote down lyrics. Or the method may simply have evolved from his uncanny gifts and insight. Had he worked any other way, however, more material would have been left behind for exploitation after his death.

On different occasions and in different interviews, Bob often said, "If Jah hadn't given me a song to sing, I wouldn't have a song to sing. The song comes from Jah, all the time."

Bob was a happy man at this stage. He was truly enjoying life away from the daily Hope Road pressure. With Cindy at his side in London, he was making progress with his work. Around this time, he offered Blackwell *Babylon by Bus* (a live two-album release) as part of the ten-record deal, hoping that, because it was a double album counted as a single record, Chris would accept it. Bob was anxious to be rid of Chris and the Island deal. The offer, which normally would have been rejected because it involved a live recording, was accepted.

One night while we were out enjoying the London nightlife, we were pulled over by the police who suspected that the car contained ganja. Stepping forward and claiming ownership of the ganja as part of his Rasta religious beliefs, Bob was fined £50. It was an unselfish gesture typical of Bob, who felt that he stood a better chance in court than any of his colleagues. I can still remember the knowing smile that crept across the judge's face when Bob explained that ganja use was part of his religious practice. The judge wryly informed him that it was a practice he would have to suspend while in the UK.

During this period Bob also met the crown prince of Ethiopia, Asfa Wossen, who asked him for financial help in bringing Haile Selassie's family out of Ethiopia. Without a moment's hesitation, Bob gave the prince fifty thousand dollars. No matter what the costs, he felt strongly that he could never refuse a request to help the Selassie family. Helping them, he felt, was his duty as a Rastafari, perhaps even his reason for being or destiny. His Rastafari faith never wavered but only seemed to grow stronger with the years.

As a token of his appreciation, the prince gave Bob a ring that had been passed down to him through the family. Accepting it as a sign and a crowning affirmation of his faith, Bob wore the ring from that day on and was buried with it. He took the ring as a symbol of his youthful promise, an interpretation shared by those close to him with whom he had a common religious bond and who knew about his dreams and visions. The ring became an object of controversy upon his death, with some family members and friends objecting that it should not have been buried with him.

This London period had begun to worry his traditional admirers and some close advisers, who felt that the relaxed lifestyle was hurting him, that for the sake of regaining the special edge to his music, Bob needed to quickly return to Jamaica.

With the album finished, we lingered in England for another month or so, making plans for another European tour, at the end of which, we decided, we would return home.

Bob seemed to be recapturing his revolutionary mood, perhaps because of Prime Minister Michael Manley who, having won the 1976 elections that followed on the attempted assassination and the free concert, was visiting England.

One Saturday during the summer of 1977, we had a meeting with Manley, at his request, during which he argued that it was important for Bob's sake that we return to Jamaica. The attempted assassination, Manley said, had had definite links to the CIA, who wanted to oust him from power. He said that he was sure that we would want to know the true cause and reason behind the shooting.

Manley and his colleagues, according to a story then making the rounds, regarded the shooting as a CIA plot abetted by supporters of the JLP. According to the story, its real aim had been to kill both Manley and Bob. This line of thinking was also implicit in a *Penthouse* magazine article that claimed the CIA had wanted Manley out because of his socialist ambitions and his closeness to Fidel Castro.

Manley did not tell us then that the shooting had still not been solved by the Jamaican police or government. Officially, the shooting remains unsolved even today. It was our ghetto allies who, much later, would crack the case, dealing the culprits a harsh, brutal justice.

With a second European tour looming, I had by now assembled the full group in London. We were ready to start.

This would be a follow-up tour running from July to August. It would include stops in Paris, Stockholm, Belgium, Holland, Munich, Hamburg, Berlin, Copenhagen and Gothenburg. We would then return to London, break up, and reassemble a month later to complete the USA leg. We would be accompanied by the group Steel Pulse, on their first major tour.

The tour had been booked into larger venues than ever because of the growing demand for Bob and reggae music, Indeed, in Holland, the demand for tickets was so overwhelming that the show had to be moved to a warehouse in The Hague, an hour's drive out of Amsterdam. Twelve thousand fans crammed into that warehouse, creating the kind of vibe and excitement that had to be experienced to be believed.

But almost immediately, from the moment we arrived in Paris, our first stop, there were ominous storm clouds.

We had taken our usual Presidential Suite at the Hilton Hotel, near the Eiffel Tower, and not far from a park where, as in London, Bob could play soccer. Bob and I shared the three-bedroom suite with the usual political friend that we always took on tour—this time a youth from Trench Town named Lip. Rita's room was two floors down.

Bob was still reveling in his calm *Kaya* spirit. We began to make our usual Paris rounds, visiting Mrs. Carmen Parris, Jamaica's ambassador to France, who had become a close friend of Bob's. There was an Island party hosted by Chris Blackwell. Bianca Jagger flew in from Brazil to attend, Princess Caroline from Monaco. Mrs. Parris came with Laurel Williams, a former Miss Jamaica, and a young Jamaican Chinese girl named Sandra Kong, who was a Miss Jamaica Body Beautiful. It was an open secret that Bianca Jagger had her eyes on Bob, as did Princess Caroline, but Bob was interested only in Sandra Kong, who was a friend of Cindy's. Ultimately, a relationship developed between Bob and Sandra, who fitted in with his recent mellow and loving mood.

The storm clouds, however, gathered and became ever and ever darker.

The day after the party, Bob had woken up early as usual and gone across the street to play soccer. I was sleeping late into the afternoon when I was jolted awake by a rather hysterical Rita Marley, who summoned me into the living room where Bob was sitting with his foot propped up. Rita went over to Bob and, pointing to his toe, cried, "Look ya Don, look ya, look how Bob toe a rotten off." I took a look at the toe, which was still sweaty from soccer. Bob explained that his toe had been this way for many, many years, ever since he had kicked it one day in Jamaica during a soccer game. He explained that every now and then it would hurt and open up and then it would heal, and he kept insisting, "Rita Marley, nothing don't wrong with me toe."

But Rita insisted that I get a doctor, that something was terribly wrong.

Because Bob had played soccer almost every day in London for the past six months, I was inclined to believe him when he assured Rita, "Nothing don't wrong with mi toe Rita Marley, every time I play soccer it sweat." Perhaps I should have heeded Bob. But I didn't. Instead, I went to get a doctor.

It was 6 p.m. when I got ahold of the doctor, who came to the suite, examined Bob's toe, and said he would return the next day to take care of it.

I put the problem out of my mind and went to get some rest and to prepare for the following night's concert.

The next day the doctor returned, numbed the toe with an injection, removed the nail, and bandaged the foot. From that day, Bob was never completely healthy again. Exactly thirty days after this minor surgery, he would be diagnosed with melanoma cancer in that toe.

We finished the tour with Bob's toe in bandages.

It was a long and taxing tour for Bob, and when the European leg had ended, during the thirty-day break before the USA segment began, he left for Delaware to stay with his mother.

In Delaware, Bob again indulged his passion for playing soccer. And the toe did, indeed, seem to have healed during the layoff while we toured. But it hadn't really. A scab had formed only on the top.

Predictably, Bob hurt the toe again. This time he became concerned because the new injury was not only painful, it refused to heal. He broke this news to me by telephone as he was informing me that Claudie Massop was now out of jail and headed for London. He told me that he had decided to go to London and meet with Claudie and others to discuss the possibility of bringing Jamaica's political factions together and starting a peace process.

From London a few days later, he called to say that he was dealing with Claudie Massop and asked me to wire him a sum of money so suspiciously large that I began to wonder if he was being held for ransom. But when I checked, I found that he was not a hostage, that it was, instead, his revolutionary spirit at work again. Apparently Bob had decided that to defeat Babylon, he would have to bring the warring political parties in Jamaica together in a peace concert.

With Bob conveniently in London, I asked Denise Mills, Chris's assistant, to take him to a doctor and have his toe examined. Its treatment by the Paris doctor was still gnawing at me, and I was beginning to worry about his health.

Denise did as she was asked.

And the bombshell fell.

From the doctor's office, Bob called me in a panic. The doctor, he reported, had X-rayed his toe, found melanoma cancer, and somberly explained to Denise Mills in another room that it was either the "toe or the tour." In the doctor's opinion, to stop the cancer from spreading, the toe had to be amputated. All this ghastly news Bob had gleaned from listening at the doorway to the doctor's conversation with Denise.

I advised Bob to return immediately to Miami.

For a second opinion, I contacted Dr. Bacon in Miami, who had operated on my gunshot wounds. He speculated that the diagnosis sounded dubious because black people rarely got melanoma, which tends to be strictly a skin disease of whites. (Studies in North America and Australia have recently challenged this theory by demonstrating that when melanoma occurs in dark-skinned people, it usually appears on the sole of the foot or the fold of the nail.)

I called Bob back and relayed Dr. Bacon's opinion. I told him to pack a shoulder bag, leaving everything else, and come immediately to Miami.

On his arrival, I took Bob to Dr. Bacon's office. Bob had brought with him, at my request, the tissue slides from London, which Dr. Bacon examined.

To his surprise, the slides confirmed melanoma cancer.

This discovery sparked an explosion of speculation. How could Bob, a black man, have melanoma, a disease rare or unknown among blacks? Did he really have cancer or had there been a horrible mistake? The explanation making the rounds that Bob, being half white, could possibly have gotten the disease.

We had to cancel the tour. Bob would remain at my house while we worked to keep the news from leaking to the press. We clamped down a lid of secrecy on his condition. Only a few, selected people would actually know about it.

Now that Dr. Bacon was sure of the diagnosis, he admitted Bob to the hospital the following day for some medical tests.

The news, meanwhile, had sparked an uproar of continuous excitement that raged while the tests were being performed. Gad Man, leader of the Twelve Tribes of Israel, came to Miami to tell Bob that no Rasta can have cancer.

My wife, Apryl, and I did our best to cope. Gad Man continued to insist that a Rasta couldn't have cancer. He told Bob that the doctor did not know what he was talking about, and that he had nothing more than "buck toe." He convinced Bob to send down to Jamaica for the Rastafarian doctor called Pee Wee, a friend of Bob's and also a member of the Twelve Tribes of Israel, before allowing Dr. Bacon to proceed with treatment.

The situation struck me as urgent. I quickly sent a chartered plane to Jamaica for Pee Wee, picked him up myself at the airport, got him settled, and took him to see Bob and to meet with Dr. Bacon.

Dr. Bacon, who now completely agreed with the British diagnosis, wanted to amputate Bob's toe. He even suggested that there was a possibility that he might have to amputate the entire foot to prevent the cancer from spreading

Bob and those close to him made it clear that they did not want even his toe amputated, much less his entire foot. After several conversations, Dr. Bacon decided that he would pierce the toe instead and keep cutting until he got clean corners, which he would patch with a skin graft. He said, however, that if he did not get clean corners, he would have no alternative but to amputate the toe. Bob agreed to this plan of action.

The following day Pee Wee, whose real name is Dr. Carl Fraser, again went to see Dr. Bacon, who had arranged to take him to the Jackson Memorial Hospital to see the slides for himself. When Bob asked him, "What do you see Pee Wee?" he replied, somewhat vaguely, "Well, boss, if those slides that they show me are yours, then you really have cancer!"

Pee Wee, perhaps because of his Rastafarian beliefs, apparently continued to be nagged by doubts about the diagnosis and seemed reluctant to accept the medical truth. He began to wonder if Dr. Bacon really knew what he was doing. After checking, he was assured by a professor at the Howard medical school, which Pee Wee had himself attended, that Dr. Bacon was one of the ten top orthopedic surgeons in the world. In the military for some twenty years, Dr. Bacon had been the orthopedic doctor for the US Army before setting up private practice in Miami. His record was unimpeachable.

This unqualified endorsement put an end to the immediate doubts and arguments and allowed us to proceed with the operation. As it turned out, the doctor was able to save some of the toe.

After the operation, Bob remained in the hospital for about a week then came to my house to recuperate. His convalescence lasted about three months, during which Rita visited occasionally as did Diane Jobson and the kids.

He spent most of his days during those three months in my garage reading his Bible and playing his guitar. Many evenings he could be seen pushing Christopher, my recently arrived son, around the neighborhood in a stroller. He grew very close to my wife Apryl, who made sure that he stuck to the diet of liver recommended by Dr. Bacon. Because I was often away on business during this period, the gossipmongers went to work, whispering that Christopher was actually Bob's child.

He instructed me to find a Miami house to buy for his mother, whose arthritis was aggravated by the Delaware cold. When I asked him what kind of house, he said a big one like she used to clean for white people.

Recuperating, Bob continued to work on his albums and to plan his return to Jamaica. His plans for the peace concert were now complete had taken on major proportions. Fired up by Claudie Massop, he saw himself as a peacemaker for the oppressed in the ghetto.

The concert was actually a continuation of the peace movement—led by Claudie Massop of the JLP and Bucky Marshall, a leading don of the PNP—that had been emerging spontaneously out of the Kingston ghettos. The two apparently were heeding Bob's words that the way to defeat Babylon was to avoid "politricks."

Bob, however, had now become a major player in the peace movement and the single backer of the concert, which would eventually cost some US$50,000. Through his personal involvement, he became the major link between the government, the opposition, and the ghetto. Finally within reach was the unity he had been hoping for in the fight against Babylon as the ghetto's energies now turned against the true enemy. As Bob said:

> Well I would not support anyone. I'll support myself, a Rasta, you know what I mean? Only Rasta, no one else is what the people want. Everything's our territory.

It was clear that Bob wanted a revolution that would stop the exploitation of the oppressed and the neglected of the Kingston and worldwide ghettos. The gang leaders around him represented not only living products of the ghetto, but also provided a necessary tool to fight the revolution, whether it entailed a mental or physical confrontation.

He had weighed all the stories that followed in the wake of his assassination attempt and had begun to realize his own power. Prime ministers catered to him and pleaded with him. To his lyrics and philosophy, the whole world was responding. I began to witness the transformation of Bob Marley who, all his life, had preached against the evil of politicians, into a politician more skillful than either Manley or Seaga. I saw him elated and inflated with his own power as he virtually became judge, jury and executioner. I saw him inch closer to achieving his dream: the overthrow of Babylon.

On our return to Jamaica, for example, when a customs officer tried to go through his baggage, Bob turned to him and snapped, "Bwoy, give me this blood claat," picked up his things and stalked out of the Customs hall. No one said a word or tried to stop him.

The next day I received a call from the collector of customs. "Don," he pleaded, "we know Bob can do anything and nobody will challenge it. But ask him not to embarrass my officers that way."

His connections with the political hierarchy and his control of the toughest of the tough among both the JLP and the PNP—people like Claudie Massop and Tony Welch—meant that you did not take chances with Bob.

Even many of these dangerous hangers-on began to fear him, and as their fear grew, Bob became more manipulative as he found that he could get them to react to his whims. Nor was it clear how these toughs would react if anyone showed Bob disrespect. People began to treat him with kid gloves.

Among his following, besides the ghetto toughs, Bob also counted policemen and loyal fans of his music. He began to feel that he could lead a religious revolution of the Rastafarian faith and overthrow both Jamaican leaders. Although he repeatedly said, "I don't want to be nuh leader," I myself wasn't fooled, noting that Bob never failed to use his economic clout to retain control.

Some people were still reluctant to participate in the concert. One was Peter Tosh, who kept saying that he felt very strongly that anyone who took part in the concert would die. That statement turned out to be prophetically true: both Bob and Tosh are now dead, as are Massop and Marshall. Some say that even Mick Jagger came close to death.

Peter had, at that time, signed with Rolling Stone Records and was playing host to Mick Jagger in Kingston, who was in Jamaica catching up on reggae vibes. In an interview with the

Jamaica Daily News, Jagger referred to Bob as his friend. Although I had had nothing to do with this statement, Bob called me and roundly berated me about it. He demanded that I follow him to the *Daily News* so that he could make it clear that he was friends with no man who appeared on stage dressed like a bisexual(as he saw Jagger. He wanted it made clear that Mick Jagger was not his friend, but Peter Tosh's.

Although Bob and Jagger had met, they clearly weren't friends. I think Bob felt more empathy with the guitarist Keith Richard, whom he had jammed with at a concert, than he did with Jagger, who always seems to reach out for what was popular. Now he was reaching out for Bob, who plainly wasn't interested.

At the concert, Jagger was darting all over the place, backwards and forwards, without bodyguards. To Marshall, who stood and watched him, Jagger looked like money on legs.

"Perhaps we should get him kidnapped and ask for a few million ransom," suggested Marshall.

Getting wind of this remark, I passed it on to Bob. It might have been said in jest, but with the heat and fire of the 1976 elections still lingering in the breeze, we could take no chances. Bob immediately sent word to Claudie Massop and Buckie Marshall telling them "not to make any bloody claat wrong move," and to see that Jagger was left alone.

Bob said, "Hold up, guys. Hey man, don't even think it." He wanted to work again in the UK. The toughs obeyed Bob, who was unquestionably the boss.

For Bob this episode further confirmed the power he seemed able to wield over everyone.

The concert, held in April 1978, was a musical feast of the best that reggae had to offer. In addition to Bob, it featured, among others, Dennis Brown, Big Youth, Ras Michael and the

Sons of Negus, Leroy Smart, and Peter Tosh. It was a climactic homecoming for Bob. Its undisputed high point occurred towards the end of the concert when Bob brought together the warring Manley and Seaga, PNP and JLP, to center stage and made them shake hands. In a most extraordinary and moving moment, at his insistence, the two leaders also raised their hands in a sign of peace. Was Babylon ready to cooperate?

Following the concert, we put the finishing touches to the *Kaya* album and decided to remain in Jamaica after it was released. Chris Blackwell opposed the release because he felt *Kaya* was too "soft." Bob disagreed, feeling that the album would break new ground for him.

And, in fact, Bob was proven right. Soon after the release of *Kaya*, we began to get strong feedback from the Far East, Japan, Australia and New Zealand. Bob said about *Kaya*: "Maybe if I'd tried to make a heavier tune than *Kaya* they would have tried to assassinate me [again]. I would have come too hard. I have to know how to run my life, because that's what I have and nobody can tell me to put it on the line, you dig? People that aren't involved don't know it, it's my work and I know it outside in. I know when everything is cool, and I know when I trouble, you understand."

Having achieved some success with Jamaica's political directorate, Bob now turned to his African roots. He especially wanted to see Skill Cole again, who had been in Ethiopia since the Caymanas scam. He broached the idea of a visit to Africa, the one continent he had yet to conquer.

The ghetto, meanwhile, having apparently cracked the mystery of the assassination attempt, called on us, one Wednesday afternoon in June 1978, to be witnesses for the prosecution. One of Claudie's right-hand men led us to a lonely spot near the MacGregor Gully. When asked in May 1977,

"Do yu know who shot you?" Bob had replied, "Yeah, but dat top secret. Really top secret." Having faced the gunmen, he had probably known or suspected more than I did. Perhaps he was even referring to the secret message sent to him from prison by Claudie.

I did not know until then that the Jamaican underworld was so well organized. Here was the proof: the underworld had cracked a case the police claimed they could not solve. To give the police the benefit of the doubt, however, their investigations may well have been hampered by the alleged CIA involvement and their fear of the US government.

Three young men were tied and bound in the gully when we arrived. One, a young man I knew only as Leggo Beast, told the ghetto court that four of them had been trained by the CIA and given guns and unlimited supplies of cocaine to do the assassination. Claiming that they had been caught up in a situation over which they had no control, the prisoners tried to explain their involvement while pleading with me and Bob for mercy. But ghetto justice had to prevail.

The court, as constituted, listened to every plea and then passed sentence on the three accused, who confirmed that four men had been involved in the shooting.

Two of the accused were hanged and one shot in the head sometime between 5 and 6 p.m. on that Wednesday afternoon. The fourth man, I later learned, went insane over the attempted assassination and died afterwards of a cocaine overdose.

Before shooting the last victim, the ghetto generals offered the gun to Bob, saying, "Skip, yuh waan shoot the blood claat here?" As I watched, Bob refused without emotion. He was, I realized then, entering a different phase.

The grisly events of that day are still vivid in my memory: the noose being wrapped around the neck of one of the men, who was dragged away out of our sight to be hanged; the condemned men screaming and begging for mercy.

But the ghetto judges were unmoved. They had wanted Bob to see for himself that they had had nothing to do with the shooting. I was present not just as an observer—but because I, as Bob's right-hand man, had myself also been shot.

We got in the car and drove back to Hope Road. We didn't talk about what we had witnessed.

We never mentioned that day again.

It was as if that judgment Wednesday had never happened.

THE WORLD

12

THE FIRST FAR EAST TOUR

In 1978, after Bob was approached by Ronnie Burke of Synergy and Reggae Sunsplash fame, we undertook a somewhat disastrous tour of Trinidad. Ronnie had asked Bob to perform at that year's Reggae Sunsplash, and I had agreed, for a fee of thirty thousand dollars. Ronnie griped that our fee was high but reluctantly agreed to pay it. Using the argument that we were all brothers together, Synergy was always trying to book acts at a lower than usual fee.

Synergy also appealed to Cindy to intervene on their behalf in the negotiations. But when Cindy raised the subject with Bob, he told her that I was the one who handled his business, and that was that.

Synergy, having had second thoughts about the Trinidadian tour, passed the booking on to a Trinidadian promoter. The tour that followed was a disaster—lacking both proper promotion and advertisement. We drew about six thousand people, and to ensure that we would be paid, I had to spend the entire time at the gate. I collected all the cash at the concert and left the show vowing never again to be caught in such a predicament. To compound matters, the next day we were taken off the plane because unknowingly we were departing the country without a tax clearance. Getting the proper documents cost us another two days.

I vowed never again to allow Bob to be victimized by what I considered amateur promotion. Older and wiser, we returned to Jamaica and almost immediately finalized our plans to leave for Europe and the Far East.

During the pretour planning for this trip, we discovered that Junior Marvin had been deported from the USA after his conviction for transporting cocaine. We therefore had to go to Washington to get a cultural waiver before he could travel.

The tour to the Far East was, as I had expected, a resounding success. We intended to play Auckland in New Zealand; Sydney, Melbourne, Perth, Adelaide, and Brisbane in Australia; and then go on to Honolulu, Osaka and Tokyo. After that leg, we would break before taking on the USA.

In New Zealand, our arrival was marked by one of the most unusual welcomes we had ever received. A large contingent of Maoris met us at the airport and crowned Bob in a traditional ceremony held outside the hotel. Until they had performed their ceremony, they would not allow us even to register at the hotel. This episode has become one of my most treasured memories of the impact of Bob and reggae music on the world.

The following article speaks volumes about our reception in Australian.

> The Rastaman in Babylon, Queensland
> By Bill Holdsworth of the Canberra Times
> Bob Marley Concert
>
> What do Bob Marley and the people of Queensland have in common? Simple—opposites attract.

Boring. That's the only way to describe waiting for superstars to arrive. Especially when you are at Brisbane Airport and the bar's just closed. Especially since it's dark and rainy and cold. Every time you look at the screen indicator, the plane has been delayed yet again until it's one and a half hours late.

You stand around trying to glean bits of information from the record company or the tour people. Or you wander over to the other journalists to see what they know. They're holding a contest for the stupidest question to put to our tardy visitor. My contribution is "Bob Marley, what do you think of Australian beer?" Brisbane is the opener for the first reggae act to visit this country.

Then, just after 11 p.m., well past the stage when you wished you'd stayed home, the plane from Sydney drops through the murky drizzle and off-loads its human cargo. Marley strolls past almost before we realize it. The first reaction is near disappointment. The herbman is small and slight, looking gaunt and exhausted, his great ropes of hair hidden by a dull woolen tam. He has nervous faraway eyes, but where are those religious fires we'd been led to expect?

One reporter has already rushed up to him, grabbed his hand and hustled for an interview. Marley's eyes flick around as if to avoid contact but he says resignedly, "Yes, on the bus," then turns, steps into the parking lot and on to the coach. The reporter follows but meets the stiff hand of the tour manager— no interviews. Tagging behind him, we all bunch up around the doorway.

As the rest of the entourage approaches, we end up as some kind of honor guard. The women wear straw coolie hats, the men are in various military styles, faces drawn and tired, framed by hair in all conditions of wildness. They look like an advance group of the Rasta Liberation Army.

Another quiet twenty minutes assures us that nothing is going to happen tonight so we drift away. My last sight of Marley is of him halfway down the coach, slumped in his seat. silent. I think, ordinary superstars have limousines, but for the Wailers, it's Brisbane by bus.

Next day, the band spends five hours in the Festival Hall rehearsing, indicating some trepidation about this first show. Marley even practices his dancing in front of a full-length mirror. Food is ferried in from a local vegetarian restaurant, Salad Days. They found they had to supply some odd things. The I-Threes, the women who do the backing vocals, refuse to drink tap water; they want spring water.

Showtime is now nine o'clock and there is an SRO crowd of 4,500. Doug Parkinson and his Southern Star Band provided a competent set of sophisticated but accessible jazz-funk but the excitement has been reserved for the Natty One. He arrives to uproar, his Medusa locks resplendently free and flying and a magical night starts appropriately with "Positive Vibration." The day's jitters now seem pointless.

Ethiopia is everywhere. That nation's green, gold and red was the background for the BMW tour badges, it was the wool in the headgear worn by the I-

Threes, it was the mitten on the bassist Family Man Barrett's right hand. A huge Ethiopian flag hangs at the back surrounded by other drapes—one of Haile Selassie, another saying "One Love" spanned by the tricolor as a rainbow and a third showing the black Cross Brigade.

In "Them Belly Full," Marley exhorts people to "forget your troubles and dance." With Tyrone Downie's keyboards adding to the giant rhythm machine of the Barrett brothers, it would have been easy, but for the heavy security. Still, the down-tempo songs are powerfully mesmeric, the rockier ones surge with force.

During "Heathen," four songs into the set, Marley throws off his guitar, which he was only scratching anyway. Now he's free, and launches into a joyous dance, arms, legs and hair all seeking separate planes. Meanwhile, the second star, Junior Marvin, cranks up his guitar and releases a churning high-note tirade from the edge of the stage. As Marley returns to his mike, Marvin frolics behind him. All this time the pulse beat grows stronger.

Onward and upward, through "I Shot the Sheriff," "No Woman No Cry," "War" and 'Come Lively Up Yourself," the crowd begins to overpower the strong-arm security and everybody gets into gymnastics. When the band departs after "Jamming," the audience goes bananas.

The encore is even more amazing, hitting a peak on a rabble-rousing "Get Up Stand Up." We are doing just that, enthusiastically whooping and singing along,

4,500 people singing about a revolution eons from their lives. All this time, the backdrop of Selassie is spotlighted and the I-Threes point towards it.

The band has gone again and the houselights are up, but the noise barrage indicates that no one is going home. Backstage, they're speechless, ecstatic, slapping each other. The last encore lasts half an hour and they take to the stage for yet another twenty minutes. Island Records rep Phil Cooper says Bob's never done two encores before.

After the concert, hundreds of fans wait at the stage door to cheer. Junior Marvin's showmanship won a lot of attention and he's busy shaking upthrust hands from the bus window. Up front, others are passing around a joint offered up by an appreciative fan and drinking cans of XXXX. ("What do you think of Australian beer?") Later, when two of the band taxi back to the hall, someone else gives them a cigarette and apologizes, "Sorry, it's only the mild Queensland stuff."

The morning after, I'm standing in the same airport lounge to see Marley leave. Still tired, by now with flashing eyes, he roams around chatting, laughing, playing with a short ivory-tipped cane. He picks up a paper, reads about the Zimbabwe elections, then crosses to the book stand, where he finds a copy of Lobsang Rampa.

Like all the reporters who have spoken to him, I have trouble with his rastaspeak. He is friendly, sincere and patient but he easily negotiates his way through questions he feels do not require answers.

Your religion is obviously an inseparable part of your music. How do you feel about white audiences here getting off on your music but ignoring the message?

Marley: How do you know they're not getting the message?

Well at the concert last night, I asked several people who Selassie was, and they didn't know.

Marley: Do you know who he is?

Until his death, he was the emperor of Ethiopia.

Marley: To you. It is better that some people do not know who he is than for some to know him in the wrong way. If a guy knows him as he used to be, he will never really know him. He is God Almighty.

Phyllis Diller has just arrived and is climbing into a Rolls-Royce. I'm on my way to the bus stop after waving the Wailers good-bye, carrying my very own memento of the Rastaman. It is a fragment of paper on which he's written "Rastafari is God. Love, Bob Marley."

Topping even our success in Australia and New Zealand was our overwhelming reception in Japan where, despite the language barrier, the tour shattered records and indelibly imprinted Marley and reggae on the Japanese music world—leaving behind an impression that continues to grow and to underscore Bob's words: "Unity is the world's key, and racial harmony. Until the white man stop calling himself white and the black man stop calling himself black, we will not see it. All the people on earth are just one family, and so my music defends righteousness. If you're black and you're wrong, you're wrong; if you're white and you're wrong, you're wrong; if you're Indian and you're wrong, you're wrong. It's universal."

Our final stop, before breaking up in Miami, was Nassau, Bahamas, where I had arranged a concert in aid of Bahamian children and in honor of my longtime friends, the Knottages. Although a huge success, with the crowd swelling the limits of Soldiers Field, the concert nevertheless created a serious political backlash because Rastas are, in the Bahamas as in other Caribbean countries, a no-no. Ruby Knottage became subsequently known as the "Mother of Rasta," a label unfairly pinned on her by the opposition party jockeying for political clout with the local population.

One of our longest tours having come to a close, we now needed the time to rest and recover. No one needed rest more than Bob, who was looking increasingly tired. His replies to the continuous inquires were, as usual, philosophical:

> "My life here, this flesh; me have to live. Me never say there was no fear of death but mi nuh deal with death. Me have no time to risk this flesh too much 'cause it's this mi have to do it in." (November 1979)

13

THE BREAKUP

Shortly after the tour, Bob called me in Miami to say that he wanted to visit Skill Cole in Ethiopia immediately after Christmas. I applied to the Ethiopian Embassy for visas but was refused after a two-week wait. Bob was undeterred: he insisted that we could get visas if we went to Kenya. But when we reached Kenya, the answer from the Ethiopian Embassy after an interview was the same: no visas.

Bob reacted uncharacteristically by storming out of the interview and taking off alone down the main street. By the time I caught up with him, he was standing in front of an art store talking to a man who claimed he could get us visas. My reaction as a worldly businessman and former street hustler was skeptical. I asked myself silently, "Whey the man no just beg Bob him two hundred dollars and make us go on?" Instead, for the sake of a measly two hundred dollars, we would now have to slog back to the embassy for another disappointment. But Bob insisted. One way or the other, he was determined to get to Ethiopia.

At the embassy, the man walked up to the official who had turned us down earlier and addressed him in Arabic. Without any further questions, the official stamped our passports with visas.

Our benefactor turned out to be one of the original Rastamen who had left Jamaica long before Bob was born and who was now married to the sister of the Ethiopian ambassador. He explained that he had not recognized Bob but on overhearing him muttering under his breath, "Blood claat," had asked, "You are a Jamaican?" to which Bob had replied, "Yes is mi name Bob Marley." On learning about Bob's troubles with the embassy, he decided to help us.

I was impressed then; I am impressed now. Bob could accomplish anything. He made a statement in one of his songs: "You ah go tired fe see me face and you can't get me out of the race," and today I'm convinced that his interpretation of reggae will always be remembered, will outlast all others. His faith in Jah as his provider and guidance was always unshakable.

As he once said, "I've been here before and will come again, but I'm not going this trip through, for there are two roads. One is life and one is death. And if you live in death then you must be dead. And if you live in life you must live. The way the mouth say, make you live."

The incident in Kenya is a small but classic example of his power as shaman and superstar.

Armed with our visas, we set out to visit Skill in Ethiopia, where he had fled after the Caymanas scam. The visit would also be a fulfillment of Bob's dreams of visiting Sashemene. During the build-up to the trip, I also discovered that Bob was secretly planning to build a four-million-dollars development for the Rasta community in Ethiopia.

We were accompanied on the trip by a ghetto youth named Lip, whose girlfriend has the only picture of Bob in

Ethiopia—a Polaroid shot taken by Lip showing Bob standing under an Ethiopian sycamore tree. Lip was later to meet a tragic death in Jamaica, where he was gunned down by political partisans.

Malachi also came with us from London. It was Malachi who never ceased preaching the glory of Ethiopia and who Bob thought would be the most suitable companion to take on the trip. But after only two days, Malachi began complaining about wanting to go "home" to England. Hearing a Elder calling England his home, Bob said with disgust, "Then Malachi after me spend all my money bring yu to Africa, yu a talk bout England as home and want to return to London."

We spent four days in Ethiopia buying art and other cultural mementos and mainly following Bob throughout Addis Ababa.

Now that I think about the trip, it strikes me as having been Bob's pilgrimage to his spiritual homeland. He described his reaction to the Ethiopian experience this way, "Boy I really get the recharge from Ethiopia because the song 'Zimbabwe' was written in a land called Sashemene. So you can say it is a full recharge, that, and when the song came out it [Independence] just happen. So can you imagine if it was in Ethiopia where you wrote all your songs, then nearly every song you write could happen, then maybe somebody would say 'Boy, he is a prophet.'"

Our breakup occurred after this fateful trip.

Although it was not generally known, my management of Bob was not an exclusive arrangement. I continued to represent other performers including Jimmy Cliff, whose career at Island Records reflects Chris Blackwell's typical style of dealing with artistes.

In 1979, I bought Jimmy Cliff's published work for forty thousand dollars. No one else wanted it. I also began to resuscitate his career, which had gone downhill.

For some fifteen years, Jimmy Cliff had been a part of Island Records. His career, which had been sagging badly, needed rebuilding, and we began by working on the album, *I Am the Living*. Deniece Williams, whom I was then seeing (my wife Apryl and I having been divorced for some time), helped me with production. Alec Willis, who had once worked for Earth Wind and Fire, assisted. This album jump-started Jimmy's career and eventually went to the Top 50, becoming his first real success since "The Harder They Come."

Once again I got into arguments with Chris Blackwell who, I discovered, after ten years, had still not paid Jimmy for his African tour. Eventually I got Jimmy £12,000.

The seeds of the breakup between Bob and me were planted on our second tour to LA when I was approached by a guy called Bobette, then a stranger to me, who had once worked for James Brown. Later I learned that Bobette was regarded in the business as an informer. Rumors about his unreliable behavior, in retrospect, should have made me more careful.

Because Bobette was then representing the family of President Omar Bongo of Gabon, I assumed he was genuine.

We had played at UCLA the previous Saturday to a sellout crowd of fourteen thousand. The night I met Bobette, we would be playing a benefit concert at the Roxy for Sugar Ray Robinson, which had quickly sold out at one hundred dollars per ticket.

That night Bobette turned up with two girls, said to be the daughters of the president of Gabon, one of whom was named Pascalene. They wanted to come backstage to meet Bob and to invite him to a private dinner. Because I was always protective of Bob's privacy on tour and made every effort to limit the hangers-on, I resisted at first, but eventually relented. I introduced Bob to Pascalene, who invited him to a dinner at their Beverly Hills house.

Bob, however, would not eat just anybody's cooking. On those rare occasions when we ate out, our host always had to hire a special lady to do the cooking. The only person in L.A. whose food Bob would eat other than that of his own traveling cooks, was a lady called Delrose, who owned a restaurant called "Delrose's Jamaican Restaurant." He agreed to go to dinner only if Delrose cooked his food.

Pascalene's motives were obvious: She was clearly attracted to Bob. Indeed, after his death, she named her first child Nesta, Bob's middle name. Not only was she personally interested in Bob, she also told us that she wanted to hire him to play at her birthday party to be held in Gabon, with the bill to be paid by her father. Somehow she got both of us—Bob and me—to agree to schedule the performance which, because we had to charter performance equipment in LA and fly it to Gabon, came to more than $500,000.

Bobette, who by now had revealed himself to be a typical New York hustler, was arranging all the details.

As it turned out, Bobette had promised Pascalene and the president of Gabon that there would be two shows even though he was paid enough to do only one. Told that Bob would do only one show, Bobette, as an alternative, paid me a deposit for Jimmy Cliff to do the other. Where the second deposit came from I never knew.

For this agreement I gave Bobette two separate receipts: one for Jimmy Cliff, another for Bob. Bobette, however, continued to give the president the impression that two Marley concerts would be staged, and we arrived in Gabon to find ourselves in hot water with the president over money.

The president summoned us to account for the misunderstanding. I explained that there were to be two separate shows—by Bob Marley and Jimmy Cliff—and that the receipts clearly stated this understanding. Although the explanation seemed to satisfy everyone, I could see that Bob was displeased and seemed to feel that I had siphoned off some of his earnings to Jimmy Cliff. On the return flight from Gabon, I sat apart from him. Even when Rita came over to tell me that Bob realized that his accusation was untrue, I still kept my distance.

My personal management agreement with Bob being due for renegotiation anyway, the estrangement was probably opportune. I had my own future to consider and was seriously wondering if it lay with Bob. I had taken him far, but with his grasp of business and his ability to handle most of his affairs in his own way, I sensed, and had already hinted to him, that he was becoming too big for an independent like me to manage.

On our return from Gabon in early 1979, I went to Miami; Bob went to Jamaica. Our separation had begun.

Sensing the break, the vultures began to hover. Through his mother, and intermittently by phone, Bob and I continued to stay in touch, but only on strictly business matters.

Skill Cole had returned from Ethiopia and, with Danny Sims, taken over tour management. The two of them actually handled the 1980 world tour, the last US and European tours, and the later tours of the Far East and Africa.

All this time Bob should have been seeing his doctors for a monthly checkup. Indeed, Dr. Bacon continually called me to inquire about his progress. In turn, I would call his mother to find out if Bob was obeying the doctor's instructions, which included a strict daily medical diet of eight ounces of liver.

In an interview, Bob said: "They don't want to run this

thing like how I run it. Them want to run me on a star trip. But I realize my structure run down, I must rest, but they are not concerned with my structure. Dem run and plan a North American tour. I watch Muhammad Ali and Allan Cole, and I see how them athletes take care of their structure. But them people who set up the tour do not work. Them just collect the money and when night come yu find them in bed with two girls while you buss yu rass claat a work all the time."

The doctors' instructions were not being heeded—I learned that from one of my calls. Indeed, I discovered that on one occasion, his follow-up examination had consisted of nothing more than a physical given by a regular British GP, who pronounced him in good health.

Our relationship remained in limbo until Bob returned to Miami for a break after the 1980 UK and European world tour—a normal enough interlude before starting the second scheduled tour, of the Far East.

It was on his return to Miami that the scene between Bob and me, related in the Prelude, occurred. It was then that Bob led me to his bedroom in his mother's house, where he had been staying, and demanded that I sign a paper dissolving all agreements, verbal or written, that had ever existed between us. It was there that Allan, whom I had not seen since the visit to Ethiopia, actually threatened my life with a 9 mm pistol after a tussle in the bedroom, saying, "If yuh nuh sign the blood claat paper me ah go shoot yuh."

I refused to sign. A lot of screaming and shouting ensued and, although no real blows were exchanged, guns were drawn.

Glancing into Bob's eyes, I saw mirrored there a world of conflicting emotions. After the tussle, he said to Allan, in an almost total aboutface, "Now that we have everything under control I guess Don Taylor can come back to work for us again."

It was almost as if he considered the emotional explosion a cleansing experience, after which we could now resume a normal relationship.

We did not know then that the cancer was spreading. But I had a sense of foreboding that the failure of those around him to grasp his urgent medical needs had taken its toll on Bob, mentally and physically.

The latest episode, however, added to the trauma of my shooting, had firmly decided my mind. I told Bob that the relationship between us could never be resumed, that it was over.

Allan would never have hurt anyone, let alone me. Bob, I still firmly believe, did not have it within him to kill. In the heat of the moment, he was, in plain fact, just being Bob Marley, Tuff Gong—perhaps even trying to impress Skill.

Nevertheless, as a precaution, I reported the incident to the Miami police. And, knowing the kind of people who hung around Bob and depended on him for a living, I went out and bought a .45.

I ended up suing Bob for $500,000 under my contract understanding, which we later agreed to settle for a figure that included a cash payment. Bob died, however, before the settlement could be finalized, even though he had instructed his Miami lawyer to settle with my lawyer, Stephen Fisher.

After his death, Rita approached me, saying that Bob had intended to settle. We agreed on a figure which, for personal reasons, I won't disclose.

It included settlement cash of US$75,000, which Rita Marley paid.

14

FROM SEPARATION TO DEATH

Bob and I had parted but our friendship continued even though I had begun to take a greater interest in the careers of other artistes such as Jimmy Cliff. Even then Bob did not try to end my control of his personal business. By phone and through his mother, Cedella, we kept in touch.

His medical condition worsened. In September 1980, he collapsed in Central Park. His family and Dr. Pee Wee Fraser had Bob flown to the Bavarian Alps by Concorde for treatment by one Dr. Josef Issels at the Issels Clinic. I was not consulted on this decision.

Bob kept me informed with intermittent phone calls. He expressed his concern about his medical treatment and the response of those around him, family and friends, to his illness and possible impending death. He was especially worried about the wills everyone wanted him to sign.

From day to day, his mood would vary as the tumor increasingly affected his brain.

In one unforgettable call, he invited me to visit him in Germany on the pretext of wanting me to arrange a nine-month world tour. In all the time I had known him, Bob had never before wanted a tour to last longer than a month.

I almost visited him. Indeed, while on tour with Jimmy Cliff, I once came within fifty miles of the clinic.

But I never made the visit, and in a way, I'm now sorry. The fact is that I was not sure then that I would be able to handle seeing him so desperately sick. I was also feeling uneasy about his complaints that those around him, who should have been protecting him and seeing to his welfare, were not doing what he wished. My inclination was to keep away from an unpleasant situation.

Indeed, following my departure, the whole scene around Bob had not only changed but had seriously deteriorated. A whole new group seemed to have taken over, who were reportedly extensively using crack and cocaine. Under the new management by Skill and Danny Sims, I can only guess that the controls I had formerly exercised had broken down completely.

In January when Bob had left me, he was in what I considered excellent health. True, he had had the sick toe, but he had lived with that that for some three years. By following Dr. Bacon's advice and prescribed regimen, he was expected to improve.

But it was obvious that the doctor's rigid medical regimen had not been followed. Ironically, it was not long after the British family doctor had pronounced him physically fit that Bob had collapsed in Central Park after his Madison Square Garden concert.

The cancer, it was discovered then, had spread to his brain.

No one has ever satisfactorily explained, even now, why his manager had taken him to a British family doctor(a general practitioner no less—when everyone knew that Bob had cancer. I still recall how horrified Dr. Bacon was when he found out that Bob had been ignoring his orders, and how we had to insist that we be sent the medical photographs taken after his collapse in Central Park.

The photographs got to us in Miami. Dr. Bacon looked at them. They showed that the cancer was growing(alarmingly— and spreading.

Bob said:

> Hail Rasta! You t'ink anything can rass kill me? I understand that writers and people in the press are very interested and concerned about my health. I want to say thank you for your interest and that I'll be back on the road again in 1981(really performing for the fans we love. Beautiful y'know. It's Bob talkin' to ya, have no doubt. See? Good. (November 1980)

> I have gone inside myself more. I have had time to explore my beliefs and I am the stronger because of it. (March 1981)

I vividly remember a disturbing call I received in my LA office from Bob, telling me that he was leaving the Issels Clinic in Germany and returning to Miami, where he wanted to see me. In his voice I sensed a certain resignation. But in it, too, was a hint of the old Bob Marley determined to work things out in his own way—a tone I found comforting.

During our conversation, he told me that he was being pressured by various people to sign different wills but had refused. He told me that Rita had tried to make a will; so had Diane Jobson; so had the Twelve Tribes, among others. He said that he had signed none of them, that all his companies and business affairs still remained in my hands.

In a familiar plea he reemphasized what he had always said: that his money belonged to his children, that I should make sure it went to them. He asked me to meet him at the Cedars of Lebanon Hospital to talk about these issues and other matters. Once again he had, in his own way that I have come to respect, placed important decisions in my hands.

The apparent finality apparent in this call prodded me to take the red-eye from Los Angeles to Miami, arriving early the following morning in dire need of a nap before visiting Bob. I awoke about 11:30 a.m., dressed and decided to visit my office before going to the hospital.

I was discussing the day ahead with my new assistant, Peggy Quattro (now editor and owner of *Reggae Report*), familiarizing her with my routine and some of my deals, when I found myself unable to concentrate. My mind just kept drawing blanks. Suddenly, I felt as if a spirit of some sort had hit me. Looking at Peggy, I jumped out of my chair and cried, "I am going to find out what has happened to Bob."

The phone rang that minute, with the words barely out of my mouth. It was Rita. Bob's condition had worsened. She asked me to pick her up at immediately to go to the hospital.

On the phone was the old Rita I knew, concerned less about Bob, more about business. She said she was calling from the house of Bob's mother, Cedella.

I began to feel that I had let Bob down. Why had I not gone directly to the hospital immediately on my arrival? Why, instead, had I gone to my office?

I was gripped by a persistent feeling of uneasiness and dread. My mind was haunted by flashbacks.

I remembered, for instance, buying the house for Bob's mother, from which Rita had just called and to which I was now heading on a grim rendezvous. It had cost $193,000 in

Bob in relaxed mood at the house in Kingston where we were both later shot.

Opposite: The laid back stage performer hid the personality of the "tuff gong" street fighter *(above)*.

Top: Meet the gang—Bob and the team take a rare break from touring.
Below: Bob in pensive mood.

Bob was a formidable soccer player, who was more than good enough to have turned professional.

The rising star. Bob with the Wailers in their early days together. (© Rex Features).

The Lion in his element.

1978. Bob had instructed me then to buy his mother a house as big as the ones she used to clean "for the white people dem." It was in the most exclusive section of Coral Gables: Country Walk, where every house sits on at least two acres of land.

But I had ignored his instructions to buy it for cash. Doing so made no business sense: after all, the sixty-thousand-dollar mortgage cost only five percent while cash deposits in Tortola earned eighteen percent. But Bob did not care about such thinking; his aim had been to give his mother a house free and clear.

We had had a major argument over this issue, during which Bob had said, "I don't understand oonu blood claat people who work for me, I don't inna this trus' trus' business, anything I buy must be able to pay for cash." He never used credit cards. Credit, to him, was a means of slavery. He always believed that owing nothing made him his own master.

But in spite of his objections, because business was important to me, I had left the mortgage in place.

To this day I keep feeling that by disregarding his wishes, I did him an injustice. I realize how deeply important it was to him for his mother to have her own house free and clear. And here I was heading towards the same house with a sense of foreboding.

I found myself wondering then, as I do now, about what the doctor at the Eiffel Hilton Hotel might have unwittingly started by surgically removing Bob's toenail. I was filled with regret that I had not visited him at the Bavarian clinic when I had been so close, that I had not tried to help protect him against the vultures he saw hovering around him during his sickness.

I turned into the driveway of the house. Rita Marley raced out to meet me, looking as if she had lost her mind.

"Rita what happen? What happen?" I asked.

She blurted, "We have to go to the hospital right away, 'cause Bob is dying, and he will not tell anyone anything, and he wants to see you so we have to go."

I drove as fast as I could to the hospital. We hurried upstairs to his room.

But I was too late. Bob had just died.

My business side took over. I contacted Grange Funeral Parlor in Miami to prepare the body for burial. I made arrangements for the services that would be held both in Miami and Jamaica. His death ignited arguments about who should be put in charge of what, about who should get what. I was upset, grieving, confused. But I had to muddle through as best as I could to ensure that Bob's last wishes were fulfilled.

The task ahead was not going to be easy(I knew that immediately from the vibes. Yet somehow I felt the hand of Bob was at work. Was he now sitting back and laughing at the antics of the hangers-on and scroungers?

His death actually has had a profound effect on my life(that is a truth I have only recently begun to face.

Bob Marley was important to me, not only as a business partner, but as a friend who always placed an enormous trust in my judgment. We had had an argument only once, about the Gabon concert, and it had been triggered by devious, toadying minds. Even though, at the time of his death, our lawyers were battling in court over royalties due me, he had still not removed my control of his estate, of his accounts.

We had even discussed the possibility that I would one day take over the Island contract and publishing rights from Danny Sims.

In the life of Bob Marley, without a doubt, I was the only insider. He did not make a move without telling me. Even if he slept with a woman he would call and say, "Don, boy, I slept with such and such a girl last night." I knew his moves at all times. I always knew where to find him, and he, where to find me.

Rita was not involved in Bob's financial and business affairs. She did not even know his account numbers. No matter how Bob and I might have fought, it was my name that remained on his current accounts—not Rita's, not his mother's, not his children's, only mine.

His death hit me hard.

I began to grapple with the loss of a person I had dearly loved.

SCAVENGERS

15

PASSING ON THE ESTATE — RITA AND ME

It was not a smooth road after Bob's death. Different forces quickly began exerting their own influences and making competing demands.

I asked Diane Jobson for advice on what to do about Bob's estate. She advised me to turn over the money to the attorney general in Jamaica to be held for Bob's children. Rita Marley disagreed, arguing that if I resigned and turned over the estate to a Jamaican administrator, because of the government's inept bureaucracy, the children would get nothing. I wanted the children to have the money, so I said, "OK, leave it with me and let me think about all the different factors and persons that would be entitled." I was, of course, referring to such persons as Rita Marley, Mrs. Booker, Diane Jobson and the children.

After the funeral services, I would listen carefully to every viewpoint and deal with every claimant individually.

In Jamaica, the new government(Eddie Seaga having given Michael Manley a resounding beating at the 1980 polls— offered Bob a state funeral. The family accepted the offer, and I made the arrangements through Babsy Grange, a minister of state in the prime minister's office.

Rita said she had to have access to money in the interim, so I released to her approximately four hundred thousand US dollars from the Island Records account in New York. She asked for another one million US dollars, and consenting to her request, I authorized by a fax to our lawyer in Tortola the release of this sum to Rita Marley. I also requested legal advice as to how to proceed with the transfer.

Rita, being inexperienced, asked for my help in setting up an account. I flew with her to Nassau where we went to the Bank of Nova Scotia's main branch on Bay Street to meet with a Mr. Roy Curry whom I always dealt with (I myself also had an account there). With his help, we made the necessary arrangements, and the money was transferred to Rita's account from the Barclays bank in Tortola.

Rita had her first million dollars of Bob's money.

She immediately began flying family and friends from all around the world for the funerals. A week later, the first funeral service would be held in Miami at the house Bob had bought for his mother. Four or five days after that, the official state funeral would be held in Jamaica.

Our arrival in Jamaica for the state funeral was fraught with tension and excitement, coming on the heels of the bloodiest election in Jamaica's history, with about eight hundred political killings. The peace concert, I guess one could say, had not worked.

The usual arguments developed over the official funeral that was being officiated by the very "Babylon" with which Bob had never been in tune but which had now awarded him the Order of Merit, the highest honor available in Jamaica.

> Hypocrite and parasite
> Will come up and take a bite

And if night should turn to day
A lot of people would run away...
("Who the Cap Fit")

The ecumenical service saw the joint participation of church, state, the Twelve Tribes, and the Ethiopian Orthodox Church. If only for a day, I guess in a way Bob had indeed brought everyone together.

To show respect for Bob, the whole country turned out, lining the roads for a full sixty miles as the procession wound to Nine Miles in St. Ann, where he was to be buried. Michael Manley got a rousing reception at the funeral service, creating some problems for me with the new government, as some suggested (perhaps Rita herself, who was becoming very close to Babsy Grange and Eddie Seaga) that I had something to do with it.

Maybe my dislike for some of the JLP politicians was showing.

After the state funeral in Jamaica, I flew back to Miami to await the return of Rita Marley so that we could discuss transferring Bob's estate to her.

Mrs. Booker, meanwhile, made it clear to me that she did not trust Rita and that she felt concern at being left out of the decision making regarding Bob's assets. I recall her telling me that she needed about three thousand dollars a month to live on, which I persuaded Rita to give her. Mrs. Booker had actually hinted that her preference was to have Cindy Breakspeare, not Rita, head the estate. Her comments about Rita were always the same; "So she black, is so her heart black." Several times on and off, she had said this, especially when she was upset. Cindy, however, was not an option, my lawyer having advised that because Rita was legally Mrs. Marley (even though I knew the real nature of the relationship), I could put the estate in her name, but in no one else's.

Rita intimated that, because of existing currency restrictions, she did not want to bring the entire estate into Jamaica. I told her that I would be satisfied if she opened Bahamian accounts in each of the children's names, appointed their mothers as trustees, and then transferred their fair share into the accounts. I was still, as always, trying to ensure that the money and the estate would go to the children. Rita said that was fine with her.

About two months after Bob's death, Rita and I went to Nassau. We visited my Bahamian attorney, Mrs. Ruby Knottage, whose firm was then Knottage and Miller. I reviewed my proposal with the lawyers, and Mrs. Knottage helped advise Rita. We then went to the bank and opened accounts of about ten thousand dollars each in the names of all the children. After I had resigned and nominated her as president, Rita was supposed to transfer the rest of the money into the accounts. It was also agreed that Rita would take the books to Ruby Knottage, which I believe she did.

I then started a six-month trek of introducing Rita to all the people involved in Bob's affairs, and putting everything into her hands. In the process, we made several trips around the world.

One particular trip to Los Angeles we made because of Bob's publishing contract.

The right to administer Bob's publishing companies (separate and apart from his management and recording companies) had run out prior to his death and, because of his illness, had never been renewed. So I took Rita to Los Angeles to meet Mr. Freed, head of the A&M recording company. I had begun to deal with A&M some eight to ten years before, and we had developed a good working relationship. David Steinberg accompanied me on that trip, during which I renegotiated the contract, which now provided for Rita to get a one-million-US-dollar advance immediately with the proviso that each time a record was released and the advance recouped, depending on its sales, A&M would re-advance another hundred thousand to a million dollars.

Since no one at the time could accurately determine Bob's worth or how fast money would come in, we had to base our numbers on estimates. (In fact, it turned out that within thirty days of making it, A&M was able to recoup the one million dollars advanced to Rita. The brisk sales clearly reflected the value of Bob Marley and his music, a fact many now acknowledge.)

At all these meetings, David Steinberg was present, and while awaiting closure of the deal, the three of us stayed at the Westwood Marquis Hotel.

I should note that David, whom Bob and I had always used, had never been very close to either one of us. Before Bob's death, David had been making only about ten thousand dollars a year from our account. In less than a year, however, he was being paid hundreds of thousands by Rita, which I thought strange. He seemed to have taken control of Rita. Always I have had this lurking feeling about Rita, that she had a mental quirk about white people that Bob did not share. I guess that is how they were able to deal with her.

After confirming the agreement, we all went out to Beverly Hills for dinner at Mr. Chow's restaurant, a restaurant popular with people in the music industry. It was also owned then by the president of A&M, Jerry Moss, with whom we had just completed the deal. Our party included Maynell, an attorney whom I was dating at the time; Brenda Andrews, vice-president of Irvin Almo Music; and Rita and David. It was the kind of night that remains with you forever. I think the bill came to about four thousand dollars with all the wine and champagne.

After dinner, we all returned to the hotel to await the paperwork and the check.

Leaving the rest of the party at the hotel, Maynell and I went to On the Rocks, a famous club on Sunset Boulevard where all the big names hang out. It was, in fact, the club that John Belushi was at just before he died. Its owners, Elmer Valentine and Lou Adler—Lou had developed the career of Carole King—were friends of mine. It was an exclusive, private, key club. You could not buy your way in, you had to be chosen, and when chosen as a member, you were given keys.

That night, for the first time and perhaps for no other reason than the company I was with, I was encouraged to use cocaine. Although cocaine had always been around, I had always steered clear of it. On this night, however, I took a little that was offered on a plate.

After about two hours at the club, we left for Maynell's apartment in Beverly Hills where we had sex, the greatest sex I had ever had; those who have experienced sex on cocaine for the first time will appreciate what I am talking about. But after that first time, however, the sensation is never really quite as ecstatic again, and the initial pleasure, no matter how you hard and vainly you try, can never be recaptured.

The following day Rita, David and I went back to the company and picked up the million-dollar check. Pleased and smiling, Rita went shopping. For putting that deal together, A&M paid me thirty-five thousand dollars. I took no commission from Rita Marley.

That night I went to a friend's house for dinner. Cocaine had been sprinkled on the food, unknown to me, and eating it made me high and paranoid. I returned to the hotel in such a state that I had to be taken to a hospital where the doctors, recognizing my problem, gave me Valium and sent me home.

Those two nights marked my first brush with cocaine and led to an addiction that would later get out of hand. I used cocaine after that fairly heavily for some three years before I grasped its damaging effects. I have not used it for about five years now.

It was about this time that Rita made me listen to what she called the "deceivers" tape. While at the Issels Clinic, Bob had apparently left a tape recorder running under his bed, capturing remarks that must have deeply hurt and alarmed him. The remarks on the tape ranged from, "Why him no hurry up and dead so we can get some of the money?" to "Im deserve it, is fi him fault!" More shocking even was the source of these scathing words. They were uttered by "insiders"(musicians, cooks, Twelve Tribes family members, people supposedly close to Bob. I now fully understood his frantic calls from Switzerland.

Rita was still anxious about whom I would pass the estate on to and no doubt meant the tape to influence my decision. But I had already made up my mind.

Since we needed a legal firm to handle the transfer and represent Rita, I suggested that we consult Beryl Murray, a real-estate agent in whom I had great confidence. She had been like a mother to me and the entire Marley family and had handled all our real estate transactions. In turn, Beryl took us to a lawyer named George Desnoes, who said he would be honored to be one of the administrators of the estate.

Attending the meeting were two other attorneys, Raymond Clough and a Mr. Scholefield, who took notes. To them I gave a list of Bob's estate holdings. Desnoes said that we would need a banker and promised to find one by the meeting scheduled for the next day. The banker turned out to be Louis Byles, an old and respected employee of Mutual Security Bank, formerly the Royal Bank of Canada.

At the meeting the next day, I revealed information about the locations and assets of Bob's companies. Byles said he would like to be involved, even if he had to postpone his retirement. He particularly wanted to be involved, he declared, to atone for the way Cecil Marley, his friend and Bob's uncle, had treated Bob many years ago. As earlier recounted, Bob had approached his uncle for a loan of £100 to cut a record, and Cecil Marley had thrown him out and called the police.

Byles was a genuine person(convinced of that, I began to feel better. The following day, the estate papers arrived from the bank, and I called the lawyer in Tortola, instructing him to draw up the documents necessary for my resignation and the transfer of the estate to Rita. Once the transaction was completed, Rita would have access to all the banks accounts merely with her signature.

In the light of Rita's history, perhaps I should have had misgivings about taking this step, but I was anxious to be rid of the responsibility for the estate. My lawyers had warned me that if I wasn't careful, I could get tangled in legal red tape. I also felt sympathy for Rita because of the harsh way Bob had sometimes treated her. Additionally, I felt confident that the consortium set up with the bank and the lawyers would honor Bob's wishes.

After the transfer was complete, Rita, David Steinberg and

Marvin Zolt distanced themselves from me(certainly not to my surprise. Rita continued to try to involve me in insubstantial matters, but I really didn't care, because I was heeding the advice of my lawyers to proceed carefully and stay far away from the estate.

I drifted away from involvement in estate business, even though Rita tried to hire me for another six months to help settle some final issues. I told her that there wasn't enough money in the world to pay me for that job. I would do it only for Bob Marley. If she wanted my services on other matters unrelated to the estate, on the other hand, she would have to pay my normal commission.

She hired me, with this understanding, to try and get a recording contract for the Melody Makers. I brought them to Los Angeles and landed them a contract with EMI USA Records, getting them an advance of a quarter of a million dollars on their first album.

The leopard, however, hardly ever changes its spots, and once the recording contract was signed, Steinberg and Rita did me out of a commission due on the publishing side by purposely and successfully undermining me with EMI. Nor was I paid commission on the second album Ziggy Marley cut for EMI even though I had single-handedly persuaded my friend of fifteen years, Grammy winner Thom Bell, to work on the project.

During the course of the ensuing months, a closeness developed between the major players now involved with the estate. For example, on a trip to Nassau to check on the opening of the children's accounts, I was struck by the fact that Steinberg and Zolt were roommates. That the two of them could share a room I found surprising, especially since about nine years before, when Steinberg was Thom Bell's lawyer and

Zolt was our accountant, they had had a serious disagreement resulting in name calling.

On Steinberg's advice, I also learned, Rita had formed Rita Marley Music to be located in the Netherland Antilles and intended to be the management company for the Marley estate. Tortola struck me as a more logical and less expensive choice, and I expressed this opinion. For example, Steinberg said that forming this company would cost thirty thousand dollars. Yet fourteen hundred dollars was the most I had ever paid in establishing any of the offshore companies for Bob in Tortola. After signing the papers, I told Rita that I wanted one of the two of us to go to Curacao to check on the lawyers and people who would be running the company. She agreed but never did this. However, by now it became clear to me Rita Marley Music was being quickly set up so that all future payments from Bob's music could be deposited in its accounts.

I had now physically turned over everything to Rita and the bank. It only remained for final sanction from the court to make Rita legal administrator of the estate.

Rita and her partners were forced to tolerate me and go through the motions of consulting me because a decision from the court was still pending—that was clear. They didn't want me to object to their plans. But objecting was the farthest thing from my mind. I simply wasn't paying detailed attention.

Yet I continued to find the apparent closeness between Steinberg, Zolt and Rita odd. They made frequent trips to Jamaica, Miami and Nassau; they were always having closed-door meetings.

I had originally set up the contract between Bob and Blackwell to ensure its expiration if Bob died. Blackwell would then be left with nothing more than the ten albums Bob had delivered. Fifteen years after their dates of release, the albums would revert to the estate. Chris would own nothing except what Bob had delivered and already recorded under the terms of the Island contract. Bob and I had, in fact, agreed that if Chris ever raised any objections about the contract, Bob would disclaim knowledge of its provisions on the grounds that I, not he, had signed it.

Yet, as I later discovered, Rita soon gave Blackwell, Steinberg and Zolt the first album that came out after Bob's death as well as rights to any unrecorded material Bob had left behind. For payment of a measly million dollars, she signed a contract to this effect and transferred rights I would not have given away—doing the deal even before she was officially appointed executor of the estate.

Privy to all of this was Diane Jobson, who had gone from being one of Rita's most vocal critics to her unquestioning, silent supporter.

I remember an argument Bob and Rita had had when he was staying with me in Miami and she had come up for a visit. He said, "Dutty gal why you nuh use yuh name, yuh name is Rita Anderson, mine yu mek people like Don and him wife think you an me is like them."

Indeed, Bob was always reminding Rita of her subservient status. I realize now that she must have deeply resented his attitude and perhaps had even silently waited for her revenge. I remembered a song Bob wrote about Rita:

> Now you get what you want
> Do you want more
> ("Want More")

Yet it still struck me that wherever he was, Bob was laughing to himself at the greed and the scheming and machinations of those once close to him. (Perhaps he was even proving, in his own way, that he was still able to manipulate the scene.)

For Bob himself had had no respect for money or wealth. He once told me that he did not sing for money, explaining, "Is true I man no sing for money, but if money come I must get my share, and if I did sing for money I would a stop long time ago, especially from dem early years with Coxsone and the like who use fi give me only five pounds."

With Bob gone, I found it hard to deal with the sharks and hangers-on who had once surrounded him. I was anxious to wash my hands of the whole business.

Yet I could still imagine Bob laughing at the scene and waiting for the right moment to say, "Don how yu a go decide my business for me?"

16

THE MAFIA AND ME

Although I had disconnected myself from the estate and its dealings, I still found myself enough involved to be threatened by a mob hit.

The episode happened this way. The Danny Sims-Cayman Music affair had resurfaced in a lawsuit filed against the estate for royalty earnings, and Rita had asked for my help. I turned to a friend, Dick Griffey, owner of Solar Records and then head of the Black Music Association (who was to become one of Jesse Jackson's personal advisers during his run for the US presidency). Dick, over the years, had settled many cases between black musicians and the white lawyers who would financially ravaged them, and it was in his capacity as a mediator that I sought his intervention. To settle the dispute, we invited Sims, Rita and her lawyer to a meeting at Solar Records in Hollywood.

Proposing that all white lawyers be excluded and that the principals arrive at their own settlement, we informed Rita that the best solution was for Dick and me to act as mediators,

I guess Rita's lawyer, Peter Herbert, was offended by this proposal, but with the help Dick and I provided, Rita negotiated a deal to buy back all the Marley songs Sims owned for nine hundred thousand dollars.

This was one hell of a deal. Later, Chris Blackwell would end up paying Cayman Music five million dollars for the songs. Moreover, the settlement resolved a long standing feud over the falsification of rights.

Getting back the songs had been one of Bob's last requests to me, and I was personally excited at the prospect

The meeting lasted over five hours and ended with an agreement. The next day, the papers would be drawn up, Rita would pay the money, and the transfer would be complete.

But Peter Herbert intervened to block the deal, persuading Rita that purchasing the songs wasn't in her best interest. No agreement was signed, and no money was paid.

When the deal fell through, Danny reported me to the Gambino family, allegedly headed at the time by "Big" Paul Castellano and later taken over by John Gotti, blaming me for sabotaging a lucrative deal that would have resulted in big earnings. The family put out a hit contract against me.

It was only by extraordinary luck that I found out about the contract. One of the hit men happened to be a friend of an old friend of mine from my Las Vegas years, and he warned that he had a contract on me and was just waiting for certain information. My friend called and told me what was going down.

I found out about the contract when I was staying at the Wyndham Hotel in Kingston. Realizing that my predicament was serious, I called up my own Mafia connections, the Gauchi family in Florida, and described the situation to Bobby, a top man in the family and a personal friend.

That same day, as fate would have it, I ran into Sims at the Pegasus Hotel and confronted him. "What the fuck is going on?" I asked. I finally convinced him to come with me and speak to Bobby on the telephone.

In the Italian families, no one carries more weight than a real Sicilian such as Bobby, who informed Danny that he was outweighed and that everything would be put on hold pending a meeting to clarify the circumstances.

He explained at the meeting that I was right, that Marley had never been adequately paid nor had Sims ever given Marley a proper accounting of money owed to him. Danny replied under questioning that the relevant files and documents being no longer available, the actual numbers involved could not be determined.

In the end Danny's lawsuit against the estate came to trial in New York. I appeared in court on behalf of the estate. The Mafia had made my appearance in court part of my settlement with them, but only on condition that I speak the truth.

Testifying against the estate were such close friends of Bob's as Allan Cole, Mortimer Planno and Vincent Ford (Tata), all of whom Danny was able to enlist because of Rita's attitude.

Although they were really mad, the Mafia still kept their part of the bargain even though my testimony caused them to lose the case in the US on a technicality. The court ruled that since Danny had known of the scam for years and had done nothing to stop it, he was, in fact, a collaborator and therefore not entitled to compensation as he should have taken action before the contracts had expired.

I had achieved my goal, which was for Bob to keep his money, and had also made my peace with the Family.

I patched up my relationship with Danny but continued to have problems with Rita. She always seemed reluctant to honor her commitments. My deal with Bob entitled me to 10 percent of all future earnings of the estate for up to seven years from the date of the agreement. Rita countered that in the interest of the children, she hoped I would agree to my percentage being put into a pool from which all of us—including Steinberg and Zolt—would be paid. I consented but have still not received any money. Being tired of her obvious insincerity, however, I have not made a fuss.

We had no further contact until Blackwell put out the album *Legend*, which had huge sales in the US and Europe, prompting Rita to undertake a tour of the US. At her request, I agreed to help with the *Legend* tour, a thirty-day affair on which Rita splurged exorbitantly. In the summer of 1983, we played all across America, from New York to California. Bob would have turned in his grave at the money spent on that tour. For organizing it, I was paid $40,000.

Rita played her game to get back at the people close to Bob who she felt had been disrespectful to her. Allan Cole, who used to refer to her as "the gal," fell into this category.

The estate grew in value; the machinations took on more sinister and serious overtones. They even led to a planned hit on my life by Rita following my exposure of her attempts to defraud the estate of its cash resources. It all happened quite by chance and began with a call from Louis Byles.

It was about a personal matter that Byles had called, business that I had been discussing with Camille Henry, to whom he was close. During the call I asked him about the estate and was stunned to learn that it was broke. I asked him what that meant, and he said that through the Jamaican courts, he had received only two million Jamaican dollars from the estate.

I laughed at this piddling sum and began to question him further. I asked him about the seventeen million US dollars in the overseas companies—Bob Marley Music and Media Aides Limited—when I handed over the estate to Rita.

That's when he informed me that he had a letter dated 1976 signed by Bob Marley and notarized by David Steinberg, giving all the cash assets to Rita.

I told him that even without seeing the letter, I challenged its authenticity. If such a letter had existed, I, who had handled all of Bob's affairs up to his death, would have certainly known about it. I remembered then the various occasions on which Rita had tampered with Bob's signature. I remembered also Bob's constant refrain that all he had was meant for his children.

The events reported by Byles seemed to support stories, then in circulation, alleging that US dollars from the Marley estate were being used to do favors for clients of George Desnoes.

I had become aware of the illegal sale of US dollars out of the account to various businessmen in Jamaica. Behind this sale was an employee of the legal firm of Judah Desnoes Lake Nunes Scholefield, Glen Fettiplace, who was ultimately convicted of this illegality. Once he had come to me with a check for $50,000 which he was having difficulty cashing in New York. I arranged for it to be cashed by Bank of Miami.

Because of the shortage of US dollars in Jamaica, I had accepted the reasoning justifying the transactions, namely, that by selling US dollars at a premium, the estate was offsetting its administrating costs.

Alarm bells went off. Suddenly, I understood the need for the Curacao company.

Byles got very upset at what I told him. And when I hung up, I was left feeling as if I had failed Bob.

I called Rita immediately, who asked me to meet her in Nassau. She had already been alerted by Byles, to whom I had made it clear that I would not keep the matter a secret. In fact, I had followed up the call with letters to the administrator general, the then prime minister, Eddie Seaga—with whom, I understood, Rita had developed or was developing a close relationship—and to Byles and the Mutual Security Bank.

I was livid with anger at the idea that all Bob and I had worked for was being squandered. Bob's words from 1980 kept coming back to me:

> They don't want fe trick you, them want fe trick your mind, that's the thing I don't like. Yu have eyes, yu have ears, yu can talk, yu can smell and yet them want fe trick your mind. Is better somebody ask you for something and get it rather than try to trick me fe tek it. I know who God is, now how can yu trick me? I no fool.

Two days later I had a meeting with Rita in Nassau.

She started by asking what she could do for me. I told her that the issue was not really about me but about the children whom I knew Bob had dearly loved. As an example, I mentioned Rohan (one of Marley's sons) who I understood was getting only ninety dollars per month. She responded by asking if I wanted to see the money go to "the big pussy girls." I tried desperately to explain my feeling of commitment to Bob and his children, my anger at seeing smart lawyers benefit from Bob's inheritance. I was so enraged that I told her that she was also one of the big pussy women.

I knew the letter that Byles had was a forgery, and I would not drop the matter(I made these feelings crystal clear to Rita.

I proceeded to inform the rest of the family, and Mrs. Booker and I, after a discussion, decided to fly down to Jamaica to hire a lawyer. I asked P.J. Patterson (now prime minister) to represent the children. He agreed at first until the case had escalated to include a tangled host of mothers, children, and lawyers, at which point he asked to withdraw from representing the children and represent only me.

The sequel was that Rita went to trial in Jamaica in 1989, said that the document she had given Byles was a forgery, and the court consequently removed her name from the estate.

It was not long after that someone took out a contract on my life.

When I returned to New York, Danny Sims warned me that someone had been sent to Jamaica to hit me, and that, in turn, he would send someone to protect me. Maybe he offered protection because he had now become aware that only I would tell the truth about Bob's affairs, specifically the songwriters' scam.

Danny said that a mutual friend, Kendal Minter, had innocently gone to the airport to pick up a man he thought was a Jamaican ex-Secret Service policeman. The man, he soon found out, claimed that he had been paid ten thousand US dollars to take me out. Sims arranged for the man to be held until the whole matter could be resolved.

I reported the threat to the FBI. Danny and my associates, colleagues and friends felt strongly that I was in such danger that they assigned Bill Underwood to my protection. Bill would later be allegedly associated with Nicky Barnes, the black kingpin gangster who at one time had owned the Apollo and with whom I became friends. Today Bill is serving a life sentence in Indiana. We remain friends, and I still visit him occasionally, with every belief in his innocence.

I also had other problems with Rita Marley. In the court case in 1989, for example, she said that she did not trust me. I offer no comment except to reprint here the following agreement we had entered into a few years previously:

September 26, 1983

NOW AND FUTURE ARTISTS
MANAGEMENT CORP.,
c/o Apryl Taylor,
8100 Southwest 81st Drive,
Suite 201, Miami, Florida.

Gentlemen,

Reference is made to the Recording Contract between EMI America Liberty Records and Rita Marley Music for Melody Makers and the Publishing Contract between Almo Music Corp, and Rita Marley Music for Ziggy's. It is agreed that for the services performed by Don Taylor in negotiating and in closing the aforementioned contracts, you will be entitled to a commission of Ten percent (10%) of the net payments made to Rita Marley Music for such contracts. Such commission to be calculated on all forms of payments made to Rita Marley Music including credits issued or any other consideration actually paid to Rita Marley Music. Payment of such commission to be made at such time as Rita Marley Music receives payment and shall be payable for the life of such contract. You agree that for so long as you are entitled to receive commission you will be available to Rita Marley Music for the reasonable periodic requirements of Rita Marley Music in respect of such contracts.

It is further agreed that NOW AND FUTURE is bound to provide the services of Donald Taylor to perform the services here-under in order to maintain this agreement in full force.

It is further agreed that Donald Taylor will on behalf of Rita Marley Music, seek out, place, negotiate and assist in the closing of contracts for talented musical performers, recording artistes, production and publishing companies and further assist in negotiating contracts for the benefit of Rita Marley Music. For each such contract negotiated and completed you shall be paid a commission of Ten percent (10%) payable as aforesaid.

In the event that Rita Marley Music shall require any special or extraordinary services we agree to negotiate in good faith with you in respect of remuneration for such services.

Rita Marley Music agree to reimburse all travel and miscellaneous expenses incurred by Donald Taylor for the benefit of Rita Marley Music provided such expenses have been approved by Rita Marley prior to the same being incurred by Donald Taylor.

It is understood that NOW AND FUTURE shall not make any binding agreement on behalf of R.M.M. without first obtaining the prior written consent of Rita Marley.

If the foregoing correctly reflects the Agreement between you and us, please so indicate by signing below.

Yours sincerely
Rita Marley,
RITA MARLEY MUSIC

Three years later, Rita called me in West LA. It was, as usual, a call based on self-interest. She said, "Don, don't testify and bury me, because whatever problems we have, we can work it out together."

The problem was the pending 1992 to 93 New York case in which she, Steinberg, and Zolt were facing court proceedings. I responded that if I was asked to testify, I would tell the truth.

But I was never asked. In any case, she didn't need my help: the court found that she had been misled. In a subsequent New York trial, Steinberg and Zolt were fined one million dollars each for misrepresentation. They are both appealing.

The maze and confusion over Bob's estate still startles the world.

There was yet another court action, this one to examine why Blackwell's bid of twelve million dollars for the publishing rights to Marley's songs had been accepted over MCA's of sixteen million.

But Blackwell was smart. He took the line that whereas the sale of Marley's music to MCA would move its ownership out of Jamaica, his purchase would keep it within the country and the family. Rita and the rest of the family sided with him in this argument. By using Neville Garrick as a spokesman and by playing on Jamaican culture and patriotism, Blackwell won the bid.

Interestingly enough, I have never regarded Neville Garrick as intimate with Bob's affairs, although he continues to portray himself as having been an insider. Indeed, he was not even on our first tour. Garrick begged Bob to be included on the second tour that played the NORM convention in the USA. It was on this tour, as I mentioned earlier, that we promoted the *Rastaman Vibration* album.

Garrick promptly proceeded to embarrass us by being caught by customs with a powder pan of ganja. He was arrested in Miami and jailed for four days. We bailed him out with the help of King Sporty and Captain Curry. But because he was an alien, he was not released after making bail, but was, instead, transferred to immigration. For days we could not find him. He was charged with smuggling ganja into the USA, tried, and placed on probation.

Neville Garrick became the only member of the Wailers to ever be arrested. The rest of the band had too much respect for Bob to smuggle drugs.

Neville Garrick was never on Bob's account nor involved in any of Bob's business. His job was the album jackets, the backdrops and the lights. Even the real insiders in Bob's life—people like Family Man and Carly—did not know the details of his business.

Some people will no doubt think me wrong to say that Neville Garrick was not an insider. But I know for a fact that Garrick had no personal relationship with Bob Marley. For artwork and stuff like that, however, he was Bob's key man.

On the other hand, Allan Cole was a real insider and Bob's confidant. Sometimes I even think that Bob really wanted to be the soccer player, and Allan the singer. Allan had the responsibilities, and more, that I eventually assumed. He was also Bob's intimate friend. With Allan, I never really had any problems. When I appeared on the scene, he simply turned everything over to me.

After Bob died, I tried my best to understand Rita Marley. I now see that she only kept me around was because she thought it necessary. In the wake of Bob's death, Rita played the role of queen and tried to dismiss everyone, including the Wailers, and establish her own private court. She insisted on being addressed by her employees as "Mrs. Marley."

Another character in the tangled web of personalities was Bob's mother, Cedella Booker. Observing her in action over the estate quickly confirmed stories Bob had told me about their relationship. I watched her shift support from one person to the other purely for reasons of self-interest.

She started out by being suspicious and nonsupportive of Rita in favor of Cindy. She kept telling me that Rita had given her only $36,000, which turned out to be untrue. Rita had actually given her close to one million dollars. Nevertheless, she soon shifted her support to Pascalene Bongo.

Supported by Cedella, Pascalene, the daughter of the president of Gabon who had named one of her children after Bob, had made a bid to buy the estate, and had even assumed support of Cedella's entire family. Pearl, one of Cedella's daughters, moved to LA to live with Pascalene, who took care of all her expenses. Cedella urged Pascalene to buy the Marley estate and, for that purpose, brought her to Jamaica.

When Pascalene's bid failed, Cedella shifted her support to Chris Blackwell, in return for which he had to agree to pay off the sixty to seventy thousand dollar mortgage outstanding on her house.

Next, Cedella aligned herself with Yvette Morris, who had

long before established herself as a troublemaker by claiming that one of her children had been fathered by Bob. After Bob died, Yvette reasserted this paternity claim, which Cedella supported and used to gain an additional hold on the estate. The child is now recognized by the estate as one of Bob's children.

Cedella shifted with any wind that she imagined would blow her a benefit.

"Don Taylor," Bob had said to me in words that kept ringing in my ears, "you don't know my mother."

These competing parties, because they cannot buy me, all view me with hostility. But the truth will be eventually revealed.

And to the body of what has been written about Bob Marley, this book will add truth.

17

REFLECTIONS

The implicit trust that Bob placed in me, which I have never been able to fully explain, I think sprang from our common apprenticeship in the real-life world of Kingston's street university. In that world, trust is the prime rule of the game. A verbal agreement founded on trust is regarded as solid as any contract drawn up by a lawyer.

This understanding was so ingrained in me by my informal education that when I started managing Bob Marley, no formal agreement between us was necessary.

I watched his genius at work. I observed the total informality of his lifestyle, his openness to his associates and friends. And I developed a loyalty and an affinity to his vibes that rose above mere monetary value. He knew that I would live by my word, that I would take no more than the share I was entitled to by our pact. I grew to feel a strong commitment to his children based upon endless conversations between us about their future. It was a commitment that I accepted and honored in my role as manager and friend.

Bob was one of a rare breed the likes of which we will never see again. We shared creative and human moments far beyond any cash value. Between us was a bond strengthened by the night of the shooting when my body protected him from the assassins' bullets.

Until my arrival, the *Catch a Fire* and *Burnin'* albums were failures, and it wasn't until I assumed management and responsibility for Bob that they took off(a fact I still recall with pride. Before me, the Island contract had done nothing for him. One of the defining moments of our relationship occurred the day he turned to me and said, "Don Taylor you know what I like about you is you no lickey lickey."

He meant that I refused to kiss ass.

I remember my first introduction to Peter Tosh and Bunny Wailer, part of the original Tuff Gong, at the first show with Stevie Wonder at the National Arena in Kingston. Although both Bunny and Peter had returned to the group to do the show, it was immediately clear to me that their large egos would not coexist on a day-to-day basis. (This show represented the largest local contract I had, up to then, negotiated for Bob: seventy thousand Jamaican dollars. I recall sitting down with Vunnie Isaacs at the stadium as he counted out the raw cash.)

Peter Tosh always resented Chris Blackwell, whom he referred to as "Whitewell." He said often that Whitewell's only aim was to keep them in slavery. Bunny, on the other hand, was more introverted and took no specific position or side in the differences between Bob and Peter. Flying in the iron bird, as he called airplanes, was his greatest fear and sometimes caused disruption among the group.

To cope with reality on its own terms, Bob set himself the task of learning. I watched him on tours as he learned from experience, step by step, gaining knowledge and confidence in the music business. He became so sure-handed at using his acquired knowledge to his own benefit that I sometimes saw him as a master politician as well as a musical giant.

There was the time, for example, after our third tour, when he insisted on flying to Tortola to check on the bank accounts. I was taking out a mortgage to buy some property, but Bob wanted it bought outright for cash. If you had the cash then you paid cash(that was his attitude. He insisted that we fly to the bank so he could actually see his money.

After he was satisfied that the money was in the bank, he said, "Yu think me fool to accuse yu early and yu making mi money. But is two tour now, and yu do you thing, yu mek more money. I nuh fool, a mus mek you do yu thing, but we equal now, as yu know me value. So me can check up on yu now. Don Taylor, member say a man can spend him life waiting on a good deal, but anybody wi gi yu a bad deal."

His reactions to the people around him bordered on the uncanny, and his perceptiveness has repeatedly been brought home to me by the continuing arguments over his life and estate.

He also had an instinctive understanding of the Jamaican mind that enabled him to immediately grasp the ramifications of any situation.

There was a time, for example, when the group felt that to control the ever-increasing crowds of uninvited guests and hangers-on who would sometimes flood the building, we had to build a fence around the Tuff Gong Studio at 56 Hope Road. We were in Rico's room shooting the breeze at our hotel in Tokyo when Bob stepped out. The conversation immediately turned to the fence and how everyone felt about it.

I was sitting on the edge of the bed; Tyrone was on the chair by the window; Family Man was next to Carly, who sat and intently rolled his joint. We were loudly expressing our views about why the fence was taking so long to go up, when Bob entered, to deafening silence. His presence among us was so strong that we often lapsed into silence until he had spoken.

Turning to no one in particular he asked, "What happen, what oonu a talk bout?" and almost in chorus the answer was, "Nothing," whereupon Bob retorted, "Oonu too blood claat lie, oonu a talk bout the fence.

"Oonu want me to lock out people and them kill me for it," (this was after the shooting). "Mi a go do it piece by piece till dem get the idea, and then nobody will hate me for it by the time it done. Oonu seem not to remember that some of the people we trying to lock out is our bredren who we grow up wid, so we must do it piece by piece."

I often think about how the Ritas and the Neville Garricks of this world have given away everything that Bob fought for, about how almost all of his life's work has once again ended up in the hands of Chris Blackwell. from which Bob had tried so hard to wrest it.

Take, for example, Ian Fleming's house, Golden Eye. Bob bought it for £50,000 through Hugh Hart. Chris's mother, Blanche Blackwell, who had been Fleming's friend, began bewailing how much the house had meant to her, persuading Diane Jobson to tell Bob that the house had been a bad deal and that Chris would buy it back for the same price. Blackwell now owns Golden Eye; he also once again owns 56 Hope Road.

I thought we had outsmarted Blackwell, but I now realize that we really hadn't. His spies were always with us on tour(people like Viv (head manager for Traffic), and David Harper (Robert Palmer's manager), who were covertly reporting back to Chris. To create the illusion of closeness between him and Bob, Blackwell used Timothy White and Stephen Davis in much the same capacity.

Yet as I sit and think about the times I spent with Marley and attempt to tell the truth as I remember it, my keenest regret is that Bob's legacy is now in the hands of people whose ownership he would have personally and strongly opposed.

His work should not have fallen in the hands of Chris Blackwell or the Japanese, or of anyone in the US or UK or Europe. Bob might belong to the world, but his work belongs to his children, to his homeland, Jamaica.

Once Bob had passed away, it was obvious that there would be a squabble for the spoils of his enormous legacy. I recall an incident that occurred to P.J. Patterson and cemented him in his resolve to represent only my interests and not those of the family in the legal wrangle that followed.

After Bob's death and before I handed over the estate, I arranged for P.J. to come to LA so I could give him an in-depth look at the music industry and Bob's potential for continuous earning.

He quickly grasped that the focus of the family (other than Rita) was limited, that they were only ogling the $30 million in the bank and missing the huge potential for income to be earned off royalties and other rights. The visit opened his eyes to the different forces that would emerge to contend for control of the estate.

As P.J., now prime minister, tells it, he returned from the LA visit to his office in Jamaica to find a seedy-looking individual waiting in his anteroom. His antennae aroused, he asked the person what he wanted and was told that he had come about the Marley estate. Mr. Patterson immediately showed the man the door. That visit prompted him to withdraw entirely from the case and remain on it only to act on my behalf.

Money has played an amazing part in Bob's life that has persisted even after his death.

One time, for example, it became common knowledge that Bob had substantial sums of money on his premises after tours and concerts. In the local jargon the whispers would say, "A bag ah money up deh."

This same kind of loose talk sadly led to the murder of Peter Tosh, who was rumored to have returned to Jamaica with lots of cash.

Similar gossip also led to an unsuccessful attempt to rob Bob. He asked me to fly down and try and uncover any inside culprits. I did identify one culpable person, who was sent into temporary exile from the entourage.

The big question, however, that everyone asks is the obvious one: why didn't Bob leave a will? Many people blame this omission on his Rastafarian beliefs. Making a will would have certainly saved the estate and the family enormous legal fees spent in the resultant court battles.

But, in fact, Bob repeatedly asked me and Diane Jobson about how important it was for him to make a will. Even on his deathbed, he was asking Diane this question.

Nevertheless, will or no will, there is no doubt in my mind that Rita's dishonesty is at the root of the problems and costs visited upon the estate and the family. She was determined to deprive the rightful owners of their fair and just rights to the money that Bob had left behind. And she was prepared to achieve this end even by forging Bob's name.

Yet as Bob himself said, "The greatest thing them [the Church] can say about death(them say you die(and go to heaven after all this sufferation. To go through all this sufferation for that! It's like after me sick go to the doctor. No, the greatest thing is life." (July 1975).

I am comforted that no matter what Babylon does, Bob will always live through his music. He will live on in the hearts of those who knew him.

And my own heart is numbered among those in which the memory of Bob Marley will always live.

But the last words are best left to Bob himself:

> "I know I was born with a price on my head, and I know that my music will go on forever. Maybe it's a fool say that, but when me know facts me can say facts. My music will go on forever."

APPENDIX: JAMAICA —
A HISTORIC CAPSULE

In 1494, Christopher Columbus, lost and floundering in his search for Zipangu, "discovered" Jamaica by drifting unceremoniously ashore somewhere along the coastline of St. Ann's Bay, not far from Nine Miles where Bob Marley himself, on February 6, 1945, would later be born. The inhabitants at the time of the admiral's arrival were peaceful Arawak Indians, who, many centuries earlier, had themselves "discovered" the island they called Xaymaca.

Struck by the stunning natural beauty of the land, Columbus extolled Jamaica as the fairest isle his eyes had ever beheld. In a later expedition, he would beach his waterlogged vessels and be marooned among this beauty for a year somewhere along the coastline of St. Ann, before being eventually rescued on June 28, 1504 by Diego De Salcedo.

The Spanish occupation of Jamaica, in historical terms, amounted to no more than a blink(barely over 140 years(but by the time it had ended in 1655 with their ejection by the English, the helpless Arawaks had been driven to extinction. No exact numbers of the perished Arawak population is known, nor for that matter, do we know the proportionate cause of death. Many Indians perished under brutal conditions of forced labor in worthless and unproductive Jamaican gold mines. Thousands more succumbed to new strains of diseases introduced by the interlopers. Scores committed suicide by hanging themselves or drinking poisonous cassava juice.

The influence of the Spaniards on Jamaica was brief but pervasive. Behind them they left quaint Spanish place names such as Oracabessa, Mount Diablo and Ocho Rios; in their first capital city, Spanish Town, they created the impressive Spanish square flanked by the first parliament building and by Kings House, residence of the early governors of Jamaica, from whose steps the abolition of slavery was announced. Today those solid brick buildings, some of the finest examples of Spanish architecture in Jamaica, remain only as fire-ravaged hulks of a vanished Spanish era.

When the Spanish landed in Jamaica, they found its original inhabitants to be a peaceful people who stood in marked contrast to the fierce Caribs of the Eastern Caribbean. The Jamaican Arawaks cultivated maize and sweet potato as their main staples and satisfied their meager needs through hunting and fishing. It is likely that they arrived in Jamaica around 700 a.d. In time the Arawaks would become renowned for introducing the Old World to tobacco, a plant they loved to smoke from their Y-shaped pipes, inhaling with intensity to produce intoxication and unconsciousness, after which, utterly at peace with the world, they would laze in hammocks, a creation they would also bequeath to the New and Old Worlds.

> Why people drink is they want the feeling I get when I smoke herb. Everybody need to get high, but some people getting high with the wrong things. (Bob Marley, January 1976)

Realizing that there was no gold in Jamaica(the real object of their voyages of exploration(the Spanish lost interest in Jamaica, and by 1512 many of their colonists had withdrawn ninety miles away to Cuba. In the ensuing years, other than growing banana, plantain, all forms of citrus, and sugar cane, the remaining Spanish did little to improve their Jamaican colony.

By 1655, however, the days of the Spaniards in Jamaica were numbered. Thirty-eight ships under Admiral William Penn, sent by Oliver Cromwell to conquer the island of Hispaniola, having failed in their mission and seeking a consolation prize, attacked Jamaica. The weak and factionalized Spanish settlers offered little resistance to the British invasion and ultimately fled from Seville in St. Ann, a site later renamed Runaway Bay to commemorate this flight.

Some fifteen years after Penn's capture of Jamaica, the Treaty of Madrid in 1670, formally ceded Jamaica to England. The island would remain a British colony for nearly three hundred years until being granted independence in 1962.

The British victory over the Spaniards ushered in the notorious era of the buccaneers during which Jamaica became the pirate capital of the world.

From their chosen capital city of Port Royal, strategically situated at the tip of the Palisadoes promontory that juts out of Kingston Harbor, the pirates raided Spanish and Dutch ships passing through the straits of Panama, plundering their goods and treasures for the British Crown. Sir Henry Morgan, the most famous of these hardened buccaneers, ruthlessly sacked the Caribbean Spanish Empire, burning the city of Panama in 1671. For his reward he was made lieutenant governor of Jamaica by Charles II and bequeathed land in the parishes of Clarendon and St. Mary.

With the death of Sir Henry Morgan in 1688, this violent period in Jamaican history was drawing to a close. Four years later, in 1692, it ended with a cataclysmic earthquake that plunged half the city of Port Royal into the ocean, killing some 2,000 of its 8,000 inhabitants.

The destruction of the so-called "wickedest city in the world," led to the founding of the present capital, Kingston, only eight miles away, on a sweep of the Liguanea Plain. With the passing of the influence of the buccaneers, the eyes of the merchants and the British realm turned to the unexploited potential of the island for the production of sugar cane.

The growing of sugar cane had begun in the South Pacific and its by-product, sugar, had already reached Europe via trade with India. Although the Spanish had introduced sugar cane on a limited scale to the West Indies, in their lust for gold, they had failed to grasp the enormous potential of this crop.

The British, however, knew better. From as early as 1640, they had enjoyed the phenomenal success of sugar cane farming on the small island of Barbados. And in the comparatively larger landmass of Jamaica, they saw even greater opportunities for the economic development of that crop. But it was a development that demanded a source of cheap human labor. Thus began the dark age of Jamaican slavery.

> Old pirates, yes they rob I
> Sold I to the merchant ships
> Minutes after they took I
> From the bottomless pit
> ("Redemption Song")

The resilience and independence of the slaves brought to Jamaica is now accepted as a historic fact. One theory even suggests that to Jamaica were shipped more rebellious and uncontrollable slaves than to any other island. The majority of them came from the Gold Coast and Benin, home to the strong and resilient Coromantees, the Ibos—red and black—and the Mandingos, tribes who had historically resisted enslavement in their own homelands. Throughout the years of slavery in Jamaica, the descendants of these tribes waged a relentless fight for freedom with an unparalleled persistence found in no other countries.

> Slave driver, the table is turned
> Catch a fire . . . you gonna get burned
> ("Slave Driver")

Wracked by fierce resistance from its enslaved, Jamaica passed through years of tumultuous and troubled episodes of rebellion, culminating in the final slave uprising, led by Sam Sharpe in 1831, that contributed to the 1838 abolition of slavery.

> We gonna fight
> We'll have to fight
> Fight for our rights
> ("Zimbabwe")

With abolition, however, came an urgent need for replacement labor, as the freed slaves abandoned the sugar estates to cultivate their own meager holdings or flooded the towns seeking work.

To fill the desperate need for labor needed to cultivate the now nearly idle land, the planters and estate owners resorted to importing indentured laborers from China and India, and in later years Germans, some of whose descendants live to this day in partial isolation in German Town in St. Elizabeth.

The arrival of the indentured slaves brought in other cultural influences, and some historians have traced the introduction of marijuana, or "ganja" (a Hindu word), to this period of migration.

> Maybe you could meditate without herb if you're somewhere that's quiet, but even if you go into the woods, there's still the birds. But if you smoke herb, the birds might sound sweeter and help you to meditate. The authorities tell you that you mustn't smoke herb because it's bad for you. Yet if they catch you at it, they'll carry you off to prison. I think it's better to be smoking herb out here, free, than being in prison. (Bob Marley, 1978)

The years that followed the abolition of slavery, up to the midnineteenth century, saw the deteriorating of labor relations, workers' wages and working conditions. These events culminated in the Morant Bay Rebellion of 1865 led by Paul Bogle and supported by George William Gordon, two of Jamaica's present-day national heroes, both of whom were executed.

> But the stone that the builder refused
> Shall be the head cornerstone
> And no matter what game they play
> We've got something they
> Can never take away
> ("Ride Natty Ride")

Sugar, meanwhile, was declining in importance on the world market. This decline, coupled with the continuous social turmoil on the island, resulted in a dwindling number of sugar-growing estates. In the midnineteenth century, five hundred plantations in Jamaica were cultivating sugar; by 1900, this number had shrunk to no more than some eighty or ninety.

Filling the void left behind by the decline of sugar was a new agricultural crop—the banana. Because of worldwide demand, the banana drew British and American investments to Jamaica and became, by the last decade of the nineteenth century, the island's most important crop. Its rise in importance led Jamaica to build a network of railways—one of the first English-speaking countries in the Western hemisphere to do so—to transport the sensitive fruit from the fields of the estates to the shipping ports of Port Antonio, Oracabessa and Montego Bay.

These developments combined to create the emerging identity of Jamaica's agricultural, political and human landscape out of the unconscious intertwining of the cultures and beliefs of the British plantocracy, the Irish and Scottish soldiers, and farm overseers (acting for the absentee landlords). Added to the modern Jamaican mix was the trading mentality of the Jews and Arabs, the resilience of the Africans, and the commitment of the indentured Indians and Chinese. These were the ingredients of the Jamaican personality that would be described to in later independence years by the motto, "Out of many, one people."

> Some are leaves, some are branches,
> But I and I are the root.
> ("Roots")

With the birth of the modern Jamaican nation came a need for the voice of the people. And at the turn of the century, the voice emerged in the form of a short, stout, black Jamaican from St. Ann (the parish of Bob Marley's birth). It was the voice of Marcus Mosiah Garvey and one that would have a deep and lasting impact on Bob's own life.

Marcus Garvey was born in St. Ann's Bay in 1887. He left Jamaica at the age of twenty-nine a well-read, self-educated man whose strong beliefs were rooted in his slogan, "Africa for the Africans." This axiom motivated his Back to Africa Movement that was launched in New York in 1917, with his founding of the Universal Negro Improvement Association (UNIA) in Harlem. Bidding farewell to his native Jamaica in 1916, Garvey's parting words, "Look to Africa for the crowning of a black King; he shall be the redeemer," were prophetic.

For Garvey and the disenfranchised blacks of the world, the UNIA represented the hopes and aspirations of the awakened Negro.

> Our desire is for a place in the world, not to distort the tranquillity of other men, but lay down our burden and rest our weary backs and feet by the banks of the Niger and sing our songs and chant our hymns to the God of Ethiopia. (Marcus Garvey)

By the 1920s, Garvey's preaching of a black God had become entwined with a rising appreciation for the glory of Ethiopianism. His words took on strength and meaning that awakened the spirit of oppressed and disenfranchised blacks. Garvey soon became the most powerful leader among the black masses of the USA and, indeed, the world.

The ends you serve that are selfish will take
you no farther than yourself, but the ends you
serve that are for all in common, will take you
into eternity. (Marcus Garvey)

Garvey's impact was irresistible and worldwide. Through
his newspaper, the *Negro World* with its battle cry, "One God,
One Aim, One Destiny," he inspired the development of black
awareness movements throughout the USA and Jamaica. But
his message, "Africa for Africans," along with his prophetic
words, "Look to Africa for the crowning of a black King; he
shall be the redeemer," although sowing the seeds of black
pride and dignity within the minds of many, were still not fully
accepted in his homeland.

A good man is never honored in his own land
Nothing strange, nothing changed
("Survival")

Garvey's preachings and philosophies had by now been
borne out by the crowning of Ras Tafari Makonnen on
November 2, 1930. Learned black preachers and historians
could, by then, prove that Egypt and Ethiopia had been parts
of Africa excised by Aryan historians to divest blacks of their
dignity and their history—a fact Bob never failed to recognize.

Ras Tafari Makonnen was the great grandson of King
Saheka Selassie of Shoa, Negus of Ethiopia, who, upon his
ascendancy, had taken the name "Haile Selassie" (power of the
trinity), "King of Kings," "Lord of Lords" and "Conquering
Lion of the Tribe of Judah." Selassie, the 225th in the line of
Ethiopian kings, traced his ancestry back to Menelek, the son
of Solomon and Sheba.

Could not one then conclude, as Bob Marley would do later, that Garvey's prophetic vision had been fulfilled, just as John the Baptist had prophesied the coming of Christ?

> Glory to Jah the prophet has come
> Give thanks and praises
> ("Confrontation")

The die, then, was finally cast.

To Garveyites in Jamaica, the crowning of Haile Selassie was a prophecy of history fulfilled and one that Garvey in his teachings had accurately predicted almost to the year. After this revelation, the followers of Garvey hungrily clung to all of his teachings, which gave form and shape to the words:

> We negroes believe in the God of Ethiopia, the everlasting God, God the Son, God the Holy Ghost, the God of all ages.

And so began the Jamaican Rastafarian movement that emerged out of the hills of Pinnacle in St. Catherine, led by Leonard Howell, and founded on the master theme, "Peace and Love."

The overwhelming influence of these teachings and its historical facts were incorporated in the Rastafari message carried to the streets of Kingston by such impressive converts as Joseph Hibbert, Archibald Dunkley and Robert Hinds.

Predictably, this rise of black self-recognition and self-esteem was met with resistance and derision by Jamaican law-makers and society shapers, who engineered the arrest of Leonard Howell on the trumped-up charge of selling photos of Haile Selassie as passports to Ethiopia.

This reawakening of black consciousness and awareness was taking place against the background of increasing labor unrest in the sugar fields and banana plantations (not unlike that of the Morant Bay Rebellion period). It was a new era marked by the rise of a consciously led labor force articulating the demand of workers for an equal place in the sun. The labor strikes of 1938 followed, ushering in the era of trade unions and political parties. Emerging to lead the struggle were Alexander Bustamante and the Bustamante Industrial Trade Union (BITU); the People's Political Party (PPP) of Marcus Garvey which faltered and failed; its replacement, the People's National Party (PNP) led by Norman Manley; and its historical opponent, the Jamaica Labor Party (JLP).

These social and political developments forcefully emphasized the people's demands for self-recognition and a better way of life.

It was also the beginning of the broadcasting era in Jamaica. Radio Jamaica and Rediffusion, an offshoot of the independent amateur station ZQI owned and run by John Grinan, was handed over to the government during the war years to promote the British cause. With peace, the British company, Rediffusion Limited, bought out the facilities and in 1950 launched the call sign RJR, featuring such bland musical fare as Patti Page, Frank Sinatra, Bing Crosby and the Andrews Sisters.

But it was soon clear to all that the rising nationalism occasioned by independence would not be satisfied by such limited programming. In September 1959, the Jamaica Broadcasting Corporation (JBC) therefore went on the air with the intention of filling the existing void by encouraging originality and creativity that reflected the diversity and color of the Jamaican people. The debut of JBC occurred simultaneously with the rising popularity of the American stations such as WINZ and WGBS that were beamed out of Miami and boasted an increasingly large listenership. Many Jamaicans musicians would tune in to these stations to catch up on the latest blues and R&B coming out of the USA.

Independent Jamaica was born on August 6, 1962 when the British Union Jack was lowered and the black, green and gold Jamaican flag raised to the resounding refrain of the new national anthem, "Eternal Father Bless Our Land," sung lustily by some forty thousand persons. Jamaicans(young, old, indigent, middle-class, and well-to-do(by the thousands sat with a visiting princess and a prince who had come officially to hand back the country to its people after some three hundred years of British rule. The historic ceremony was witnessed by vice-president of the USA, Lyndon Baines Johnson.

It was the end of the turbulent era of colonialism; Jamaica had begun to govern itself.

Ushered into the global village of the world with all the trappings of modernity, Jamaica was still in the developmental stage. The suburban areas of Kingston existed only as a blueprint, not a reality, with the city still confined to an area bounded by the Wareika Hills and Rockfort on the east, and on the west by May Pen Cemetery and the abattoir(its bowels. To the north and south it was bounded by the Blue Mountain Range of St. Andrew and the Caribbean Sea.

St. Andrew, later to be called "uptown," would finally be incorporated into Kingston and St. Andrew, forming one city, referred even to this day as simply Kingston. Scattered and unplanned, the city would flower at its edges while leaving its core downtown area neglected and in need of urgent redevelopment.

But me no have no friend inna high society
Me no have no friend, oh mark my identity
Me no have no friend
("We and Dem")

Already obvious in the new nation was a trait that would be dourly noted by its Caribbean neighbors, namely, the arrogance and confrontational style of Jamaicans. The people had resoundingly rejected the option of Federation that had been so staunchly championed by Norman Manley. A rising tide of Independence, generated by the exports of sugar, banana and bauxite, had produced a strong economic base of reserves. The nation's treasury brimmed with cash reserves making the Jamaican dollar worth more than its US counterpart. The motto of the fledgling country seemed almost to be, "Stand back while we take on the world."

The more reflective and aware, however, understood that mere creation of a flag and national anthem was not enough to mold the spirit of a nation, that Jamaicans needed to find their own sense of history and culture, to dig into their past and honor those who had led them to this historical moment. Sam Sharpe, Paul Bogle and George William Gordon and their previously untold struggles against slavery were finally recognized and their exploits honored.

But it was the charismatic leader Marcus Mosiah Garvey who attracted the most spontaneous and reverent reaction from the populace, for his had been the voice rumbling out of the suffering in the ghettos, the residence of the oppressed and the poor.

Since the white people have seen their God, through white spectacles, we have only now started out (late though it may be) to see our God, through our own spectacles. The God of Isaac and the God of Jacob, let him exist for the race that believes in this God of Isaac and the God of Jacob. We negroes believe in the God of Ethiopia, the everlasting God— God the Son, God the Holy Ghost, the God of all ages. That is the God in whom we believe, but we shall worship him through the spectacles of Ethiopia. ("Philosophy and Opinions of Marcus Garvey")

In his life and work Bob never failed to articulate these ideas.

I am sure Haile Selassie I is almighty God— with no apologies. (Bob Marley, 1976)

The early Nyabinghi Rasta believed the Babylonian "Jesus" to be a false god, and Haile Selassie to represent the first coming of the Messiah. Out of this belief came the suspicion of governments, and a philosophy to stay away from "Politricks."

As their religious beliefs developed and manifested themselves, Rastas adopted the visible characteristic of "Dreadlocks"—the uncombed and uncut hair that demands constant care and washing.

All the days of the vow of his separation, there shall be no razor come upon his head: until the

days be fulfilled, in the which he separateth
himself unto the Lord, he shall be holy, and
shall let the locks of the hair of his head grow.
(Numbers 6:5)

This religious vow became the trademark of Rastas, who
did not drink alcohol nor deal with any form of death as they
followed an ancient and traditional biblical path, comforted
only by the smoking of marijuana.

As Bob once said,

> When you smoke herb it reveals you to your-
> self. All the wickedness you do is revealed by
> the herb(it's your conscience and gives you an
> honest picture of yourself. (September 1980)

Marijuana was adopted for usage by Rastas as part of their
religious worship in the historically and biblically based belief
that the herb had been given to man by Jah to aid his medita-
tions and open his consciousness to the world. This belief
emanates from the fact that the herb first grew in the grave of
King Solomon, hence the name, "wisdom weed."

Not all Rastas smoke ganja, but it is commonly used by
many adherents of the faith. When smoked in a chalice or
chillum pipe as a form of worship, it is solemnly passed in
strict religious observance from one person to the other as a
holy sacrament with each person traditionally giving thanks
and praise to Jah. This ritual, referred to as "licking the chalice" or "sipping from the cup," is comparable to the Christian
communion rite.

Accompanying these rituals and beliefs are teachings about
food.

> Know ye not that ye are the temples of God,
> and that the spirit of God dwelleth in you! If
> any man defile the temple of God, him shall
> God destroy, for the temple of God is holy;
> which temple ye are. (Corinthians 3:16,17)

Rastas disdain pork and shellfish as the meat of so-called scavengers. Sometimes this orthodoxy is often taken to include all meat—"deaders"—though fish is less contemptuously regarded. The total exclusion of salt, which is inorganic, completes the "ital" diet, which represents the organically undefiled preparation of food.

Over the last sixty years, the developing Rasta society has given rise to offshoots of Nyabinghi with links to the Ethiopian Orthodox Church, which came to Jamaica in 1969, and is the most ancient and historic of the Christian churches. Its literature includes the *Kebra Nagast*, the book which traces Selassie's lineage to Solomon and Sheba, and records in the Geez language the story of how the Ark of the Covenant was taken from the Jews in Jerusalem and transferred by God to Ethiopia.

In Genesis, Jah created the world through His words. Rastas would also think it necessary to shape their reality through the use of language in Rasta talk, if only to differentiate the godly from the ungodly (especially as Isaiah 11:110-113 confirms that the gathering would begin in the "Isle of the sun," which the Rastas take to mean Jamaica). And so herb became I-sence—with "I" taking the dominant role of creating a singular unified identity for Rasta. Consequently Rastas express themselves in their I-ssembly (assembly) and sing I-Ses (praises) to I-nation (creation) of Jah.

In the sixties the phenomenon that was Rasta, because of its strong "Back to Africa" theme, demanded attention and became the subject of an official government study by M.G. Smith and Rex Nettleford. The government suspected the movement's unknown revolutionary intentions and its pledges to reform the "shitstem," (system) as Peter Tosh would later refer to the conventional status quo. Many of Jah's followers found proof of the movement's genesis and righteousness in its widespread growth, in its enduring of trials and criticisms(both past and present(and in the wrath with which it is even today still occasionally regarded by the establishment.

> It's too late. . . men have lost their faith . . .
> We no know how me and them a go work this out
> ("We and Dem")

During the sixties amid the changes occasioned by Independence, the Rasta movement itself did not remain static but gave rise to new doctrines in the ghetto. In 1968 the most influential of these changes was the emerging Twelve Tribes of Israel founded in Trench Town by Vernon Carrington, a vendor of juices and herb-roots drinks.

According to Carrington, the human race was made up of twelve tribes, each named after one of Jacob's sons. Each tribe was connected with a month of the year(based on the Egyptian calendar that began with April(marked by a special color and endowed with a secret blessing.

April	Reuben	Silver
May	Simeon	old
June	Levi	Purple
July	Judah	Brown

August	Issachar	Yellow
September	Zebulun	Pink
October	Dan	Blue
November	Gad	Red
December	Asher	Grey
January	Naphtali	Green
February	Joseph	White
March	Benjamin	Black

Members of the Twelve Tribes believe that one must assume the name of the biblical tribe corresponding to the month in which one's birthday falls. Carrington, being born in November, therefore became Prophet Gad; Bob, who was born in February, became Joseph.

> "... and on either side of the river was the tree
> of life, bearing twelve kinds of fruits, yielding
> its fruit every month ..." (Revelations 22:2)

Carrington's doctrines spread widely throughout the uptowners, with many converts finding appeal in its strong anti-Christianity, and the Twelve Tribes soon became the most highly organized Jamaican Rasta sect. But its popularity alienated the more traditional Rastas, who felt that the sect with its council of pyramidal structures departed from strict Rasta traditions. Nevertheless, the movement gained such converts as Dennis Brown, Freddie McGregor, Judy Mowatt, and more importantly to Bob, Allan "Skill" Cole, who influenced Bob to join the Twelve Tribes. To Rastafarian believers of the Tribe of Joseph, the second coming had already taken place and thus the "King" could not die.

The Twelve Tribes stress racial tolerance and freedom of lifestyle and appearances. They believe that what leaves your heart through your lips is more important to the world than what enters it. Being "born again, " they await the day when all tribes will once again be gathered.

> For though thy people Israel be as the sand of
> the sea, yet a remnant of them shall return...
> (Isaiah 10:22)

This sect also takes repatriation to Africa literally, a common trend running through the beliefs of all Rastas.

> I say fly away home to Zion
> Fly away home
> One bright morning when my work is over
> I will fly away home
> (Traditional Negro spiritual used in
> "Rasta Man Chant")

Strict adherence to the Bible is taught and required by this sect. Its members also believe that the answers to all questions about life can be found within pages of the Bible if it is read "a chapter a day" from beginning to end. Bob carried out this daily commitment faithfully.

In addition to the differing Rasta sects there was, of course, the oldest established Christian church, the Ethiopian Orthodox Church, of which Bob also became a member. His cycle of memberships would reflect his life's dream, namely, to unite all Rastafarian believers under one aim and one destiny. It was a dream he pursued to end of his life.

SELECTED DISCOGRAPHY

Albums produced under Don Taylor's management

LIVE!

ILPS 9376   1975

Produced by Steve Smith and Chris Blackwell

This was the album that really launched the song "No Woman No Cry," as up until then, despite being recorded on the previous *Natty Dread* LP, it had not created any waves.

This was also the album that caused the first confrontation with Chris as he had gone ahead and issued the record without our permission and not credited the production to Bob Marley and the Wailers.

Trench Town Rock	Lively Up Yourself
Burnin & Lootin	No Woman No Cry
Him Belly Full	I Shot the Sheriff
	Get Up Stand Up

RASTAMAN VIBRATION

ILPS 9383   1976

The first album credited exclusively as being produced by Bob Marley and the Wailers. This change came with the advent of my management. Up until this time, Chris Blackwell always placed his name as producer on Bob's records.

This album was a departure from the norm and had Bob reaching wider audiences and new fields of appreciation.

Positive Vibration	Roots Rock Reggae
Johnny Was	Cry To Me
Want More	Crazy Baldhead
Who the Cap Fit	Night Shift
War	Rat Race

EXODUS

ILPS 9498   1977

Produced by Bob Marley and the Wailers

This album, which became Bob's best seller, was released after the assassination attempt. Side one is a clear response to the event. It was an emotional album for us.

Natural Mystic	So Much Things to Say
Guiltiness	The Heathen
Exodus	Jamming
Waiting in Vain	Turn Your Lights Down Low
Three Little Birds	One Love/People Get Ready

KAYA

ILPS 9519   1978

Produced by Bob Marley and the Wailers

With each album released, we sought to show the expansion of Bob's creative horizons; and with *Kaya*, brought out against Chris's wishes, we again broke new ground and opened up a softer side of the market.

Easy Skanking	Is This Love
Satisfy My Soul	She's Gone
Misty Morning	Crisis
Running Away	Time Will Tell

BABYLON BY BUS
ISLD II 1298   1978
Produced by Bob Marley and the Wailers

Positive Vibration	War
Punky Reggae Party	No More Trouble
Exodus	Is This Love
Stir It Up	Heathen
Rat Race	Jamming
Concrete Jungle	Kinky Reggae
Lively Up Yourself	Rebel Music

SURVIVAL
ILPS 9542   1979
Produced by Bob Marley and the Wailers and Alex Sadkin

In this album, Bob returned to his revolutionary roots and answered the critics who thought he had gone soft.

Wake Up and Live	Africa Unite
One Drop	Ride Natty Ride
Ambush in the Night	So Much Trouble in the World
Zimbabwe	Top Ranking
Babylon System	Survival

UPRISING
ILBS 9596   1980
Produced by Bob Marley and the Wailers

This album is in a real sense the culmination of Bob's musical development and demonstrates a balance between his serious lyrics and his more adventurous flauntings. This was the last album produced before our breakup.

Coming in from the Cold	
Real Situation	Bad Card
We and Them	Work

Zion Train	Pimpers Paradise
Could You Be Loved	Forever Loving Jah
Redemption Song	

After these records, produced and recorded during my time as manager, the albums that followed were *Confrontation*, which is listed as produced by Chris Blackwell and Rita Marley, and *Legend*, a mix of previously released hits avoiding new tracks.

Reference can be made to music catalogs that recall all of Bob's music, and the book *Bob Marley: Reggae King of the World* by Malika Whitney and Dermot Hussey can provide further details including the pirated records.

The early three albums, namely *Catch a Fire, Burnin'* and *Natty Dread*, were all credited to Chris Blackwell as producer.